#1 Teacher Recommended!

BRIDGING GRADES 1 to 2

Summer Bridge®
An imprint of Carson Dellosa Education
PO Box 35665
Greensboro, NC 27425 USA

© 2025 Carson Dellosa Education. Except as permitted under the United States Copyright Act, no part of this publication may be reproduced, stored, or distributed in any form or by any means (mechanically, electronically, recording, etc.) without the prior written consent of Carson Dellosa Education. Summer Bridge® is an imprint of Carson Dellosa Education.

Printed in the USA • All rights reserved.
ISBN 978-1-4838-7270-4
2-062251151

Caution: Exercise activities may require adult supervision. Before beginning any exercise activity, consult a physician. Written parental permission is suggested for those using this book in group situations. Children should always warm up prior to beginning any exercise activity and should stop immediately if they feel any discomfort during exercise.

Caution: Nature activities may require adult supervision. Before beginning any nature activity, ask parents' permission and inquire about the child's plant and animal allergies. Remind the child not to touch plants or animals during the activity without adult supervision.

Caution: Before completing any balloon activity, ask parents' permission and inquire about possible latex allergies. Also, remember that uninflated or popped balloons may present a choking hazard.

Caution: Before beginning any food activity, ask parents' permission and inquire about child's food allergies and religious or other food restrictions.

The authors and publisher are not responsible or liable for any injury that may result from performing the exercises or activities in this book.

Table of Contents

How to Use Your *Summer Bridge Activities®* Book 4

Skills Matrix 6

Summer Reading and Free E-books 8

Section 1: Monthly Goals and Word List **10**

Introduction to Flexibility 11

Let's Play Today Activities 12

Activity Pages 13

Science Experiments 53

Social Studies Activities 55

Section 2: Monthly Goals and Word List **58**

Introduction to Strength 59

Let's Play Today Activities 60

Activity Pages 61

Science Experiments 101

Social Studies Activities 103

Section 3: Monthly Goals and Word List **106**

Introduction to Endurance 107

Let's Play Today Activities 108

Activity Pages 109

Science Experiments 149

Social Studies Activities 151

Reflect and Reset 154

Answer Key **156**

Flash Cards

Manipulatives

Progress Chart

Reference Chart

How to Use Your *Summer Bridge Activities*® Book

Three Summer Months, 15 Minutes a Day

The three color-coded sections match the three months of summer. Your child has two pages to complete each weekday (a front and a back), taking about 15 minutes total. The activities are designed to reinforce first-grade skills and introduce second-grade topics.

Special Features

Summer Reading Fun:

free e-books, summer reading BINGO, and ideas to make reading fun

Charts and Poster:

a helpful fact reference chart, a progress chart with stickers, and a summer bucket list poster

Science and Social Studies Activities:

monthly hands-on science experiments and interesting social studies activities

Flash Cards and Manipulatives:

tear-out flash cards and manipulatives for hands-on practice

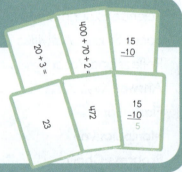

Healthy Habits Sidebars

Mindful Moments

activities focused on social and emotional learning

Let's Play Today

activities encouraging physical activity and play

Fast Fun Facts

fun trivia facts that inspire a love of learning

© Carson Dellosa Education

The adventure continues online with IXL!

Throughout this edition of Summer Bridge Activities®, you'll see 3-digit codes that connect your family with fun, motivating online practice questions on IXL, the most widely used K-12 online learning program in the U.S. On IXL.com or the IXL mobile app, simply type the 3-digit code into the Skill ID box to start "playing" IXL and earning fun awards and certificates!

Try IXL free with 10 questions per day, and learn about how an IXL membership can boost learning even further. With an IXL account you'll get:

Limitless learning
Boost learning and curiosity with over 17,000 topics in math, English, science, social studies, and Spanish for everyone, from K-12.

Support and encouragement
Get instant feedback, step-by-step explanations, videos, and more! IXL makes it easy to learn from mistakes and feel good about it.

Awards and certificates
Whimsical awards and certificates celebrate your child's achievements and keep them motivated.

A unique plan for every child
IXL builds a growth path for your child by meeting them at their learning level and giving them exactly what they need to work on next.

The learning app families trust
In over 75 scientific research studies, IXL is proven to help students make bigger learning gains and build confidence in their abilities. No wonder it's used by 1 in 4 students across the U.S.!

Ready to open up an exciting new world of learning?

Join hundreds of thousands of parents across the world and give your child access to unlimited learning with an IXL membership!

Learn more at
ixl.com/summer-bridge/1-2

Skills Matrix

Day	Addition	Geometry & Measurement	Graphing	Handwriting	Language Arts & Grammar	Number Relationships	Numbers & Counting	Patterning	Phonics	Place Value	Problem Solving	Reading Comprehension	Science	Social Studies	Spelling	Subtraction	Time & Money	Vocabulary	Writing
1				★					★			★							
2	★			★	★							★				★			
3					★				★								★		
4		★			★				★							★			
5	★				★				★										
6					★				★	★									
7									★	★	★								
8							★											★	★
9		★										★							
10									★			★			★	★			
11	★								★							★			
12	★				★				★							★			
13					★				★										
14	★				★				★							★			
15										★		★							
16					★				★			★							
17		★			★				★										
18									★	★								★	
19		★					★					★						★	
20		★							★			★					★		
BONUS PAGES!													★	★					
1	★				★		★												
2					★	★			★			★							
3	★								★		★					★			
4						★			★						★			★	
5			★						★			★							
6	★								★		★					★	★		
7		★							★		★	★							
8									★			★						★	
9					★						★					★			★
10	★				★		★		★										
11		★			★										★				★

6

© Carson Dellosa Education

Skills Matrix

Day	Addition	Geometry & Measurement	Graphing	Handwriting	Language Arts & Grammar	Number Relationships	Numbers & Couting	Patterning	Phonics	Place Value	Problem Solving	Reading Comprehension	Science	Social Studies	Spelling	Subtraction	Time & Money	Vocabulary	Writing
12					★							★				★	★		
13					★					★							★		
14							★		★						★				★
15	★				★							★				★			
16					★											★			
17	★	★			★														
18					★							★					★		
19					★							★					★	★	
20	★	★										★				★			★
BONUS PAGES!													★	★					
1	★								★			★			★				
2					★						★					★	★		
3	★	★								★									
4										★	★	★							
5									★	★		★							★
6								★				★							
7	★	★										★						★	
8		★									★	★							
9		★	★		★							★							
10	★															★	★		
11	★				★													★	
12	★								★		★	★							
13												★							
14								★								★			★
15	★									★								★	
16					★							★							
17						★						★			★				
18		★										★							
19												★				★		★	
20	★		★		★											★			
BONUS PAGES!													★	★					★

© Carson Dellosa Education

Summer Reading and Free E-books

Reading is important all year, not just during school. This summer, set yourself a reading goal and challenge yourself to complete it. You can make your goal one book a month, or even one a week! Choose a goal realistic for you.

Give some of these summer reading ideas a try to make summer reading fun and meaningful.

Read in a New Place
Read in a hammock, under a shady tree, in a sunny spot, on a porch, in a park, in a fort, on a picnic blanket, at a playground, in a tent, or any other spot you've never read before.

Make a Reading List
Make a list of books in a genre you like, books with characters your age, books by your favorite author, or come up with your own list theme. Read as many as you can and check them off as you do.

Read a Summer Book
Choose a book that is summer themed. It could be about a summer trip, summer vacation, a new neighbor, a fun adventure, or set at the beach or in a tropical location.

Be a Chef
Read a cookbook or a book about food. Choose a recipe in the book to make. Write it on a recipe card. Then make it (and enjoy it)! It's up to you if you share it!

Check Your Library
Sign up for your local library's summer reading challenge (or find one online to participate in).

Start a Book Club
Join (or start) a book club with friends or family members. Take turns choosing the book.

Free E-books!

Get started on summer reading fun now by scanning the QR codes for free e-books!

Cheetah Chases the Story

Design and Build It to Go

Language in Society

What Is Sprouting?

© Carson Dellosa Education

SUMMER READING BINGO

Cross off the reading activities as you do them.

Read under the stars.	Read on a swing.	Read to a stuffed animal or a pet.	Read while eating a frozen treat.	Read on a rainy day.
Read on a Saturday.	Read while eating lunch.	Read with a flashlight.	Read in a pillow fort.	Read in your swimsuit.
Read under a tree.	Read on a Sunday.	FREE	Read to someone on the phone.	Read on a beach towel.
Read in a car.	Read under a table.	Read out loud.	Read to an adult.	Read in your pajamas.
Read at a park.	Read on a Friday.	Read under your covers.	Read a page backwards.	Read in a funny voice.

© Carson Dellosa Education

9

SECTION 1

Monthly Goals

A *goal* is something that you want to accomplish. Sometimes, reaching a goal can be hard work!

Think of three goals to set for yourself this month. For example, you may want to learn five new vocabulary words each week. Have an adult help you write your goals on the lines.

Place a sticker next to each of your goals that you complete. Feel proud that you have met your goals!

1. _____ [PLACE STICKER HERE]

2. _____ [PLACE STICKER HERE]

3. _____ [PLACE STICKER HERE]

Word List

The following words are used in this section. Read each word aloud with an adult. When you see a word from this list on a page, circle it with your favorite color of crayon.

compare	question
correct	sentence
events	solve
half	title
long	true

10 © Carson Dellosa Education

Introduction to Flexibility

This section includes Let's Play Today and Mindful Moments activities that focus on flexibility. These activities are designed to help you become flexible physically and mentally. If you have limited mobility, feel free to modify any suggested activity or choose a different one from the list on the following page.

When we talk about flexibility with regard to our bodies, we are referring to how easily our bodies move. If our body isn't flexible, then we will have trouble doing everyday tasks, such as tying our shoes, reaching for things, or playing games or sports.

Over the summer, make a point to stretch regularly to keep your arms and legs moving easily and your back from getting sore. Challenge yourself to touch your toes daily. Did you know that everyday activities, like reaching for a dropped pencil, can help you practice stretching?

Mental flexibility is just as important as physical flexibility. Being mentally flexible means being open-minded. We all know how disappointing it can be when things do not go the way we want them to. Having a fun day at the park ruined because of rain is frustrating. Feeling disappointed or angry as a reaction is normal. In life, there will be situations where unexpected things happen. Often, it is how someone reacts to those circumstances that affects the outcome. It is important to have realistic expectations, brainstorm solutions to improve a disappointing situation, or look on the bright side of a disappointment to find joy even when things do not go as planned.

You can show flexibility of character and mind by being understanding, respecting others' differences, sharing, taking turns, and more. Learning to be flexible now at your age will give you the ability to handle unexpected situations in the years to come.

Engaging Online Practice

Bring learning to life with fun, interactive activities on IXL! Look for the Skill ID box and type the 3-digit code into the search bar on IXL.com or the IXL mobile app. Ten questions per day are free!

Skill IDs: 5UN • D9K

SECTION 1

Let's Play Today

Get your child up and moving with these Let's Play Today activities. Section 1 focuses on stretching. Stretching helps our body move in its full range of motion and helps us avoid injuring ourself when exercising or playing. Use this list in addition to or as a replacement for any Let's Play Today suggestions on the activity pages. This list was developed to be inclusive of a variety of abilities. Choose the ones that suit your child the best! Make modifications as needed. These activities may require adult supervision. See page 2 for full caution information.

Bouncy Ball Back-and-Forth:

In an open outdoor space, kick or toss a large bouncy ball back and forth with a friend, family member, or neighbor. Stretch your legs when you kick the ball or lunge to stop a returning ball. Stretch your arms if you are catching it.

The Shallow End Hop:

In the shallow end of a pool, stand on one leg and hold your arms out to your side. Hop from one side of the pool to the other without using your other leg. Switch legs and hop back to the other side.

Stretch to Pop:

Grab a container of bubbles and head outside. Blow bubbles high into the air. Stretch your arms and legs to reach them and pop them before they fall back toward the ground.

Walk a Tightrope:

Use a piece of sidewalk chalk or tape to make a long, thin line on the cement outside. Putting one foot in front of the other and with arms stretched out to the side, slowly walk on the line until you come to the end, being careful to keep your balance. Then turn around and walk back the other way. Try not to step off the line.

Weaving In and Out:

In a yard or at a playground, set up an obstacle course that is made up of traffic cones, toys, or other objects. Start with the objects spread out pretty far, and then move them closer together to make it a little more difficult. Try to move through it without touching any of the objects.

12 © Carson Dellosa Education

Reading Comprehension

Read the poem.

Pitter-Patter

Pitter-patter, pitter-patter.
How I love the rain!

Storm clouds moving in,
The rain is about to begin.
How I love to see the rain!

Tiny sprinkles on my face,
Little droplets playing chase.
How I love to feel the rain!

I open up my mouth so wide,
Letting little drops inside.
How I love to taste the rain!

Tapping on my window,
It's a rhythm that I know.
How I love to hear the rain!

Everything looks so green,
And the fresh air smells so clean.
How I love to smell the rain!

Pitter-patter, pitter-patter.
How I love the rain!

Draw a line to match each sense with a detail in the poem.

	Sense	Detail
1.	sight	tapping a rhythm on the window
2.	touch	storm clouds moving in
3.	taste	little drops inside my mouth
4.	hearing	tiny sprinkles on my face
5.	smell	clean, fresh air

 **Mindful Moment**

Think of a family member who needs your help today.
Help them do a task, and you will both feel great.

© Carson Dellosa Education

13

DAY 1

Search for this skill ID on IXL.com for more practice!

Handwriting/Phonics

Write the uppercase letters of the alphabet.

Say the name of each picture. Write the vowel that completes each word.

6.  m___p	7.  c___t	8.  b___d
9.  c___p	10.  p___n	11.  t___p

© Carson Dellosa Education

Addition & Subtraction/Language Arts & Grammar

IXL Skill IDs **C78 • A62**

DAY 2

Solve each problem.

1.   1 5
   − 1 1

2.   1 6
   − 4

3.   1 3
   − 8

4.   1 3
   + 5

5.   1 9
   − 3

6.   1 8
   + 2

7.   8
   + 9

8.   1 7
   − 9

9.   1 8
   − 4

10.   1 2
   + 6

Rewrite each sentence. Use the tense in parentheses ( ).

11. Sanja eats soup for lunch.

    (past) _____

12. Eli raced down the hill.

    (future) _____

13. Abby splashed her brother in the pool.

    (present) _____

14. The piano will need to be tuned.

    (present) _____

15. Ty will slam the car door.

    (past) _____

© Carson Dellosa Education

DAY 2

Handwriting/Reading Comprehension

Write the lowercase letters of the alphabet.

Read each sentence. Draw a picture of one of the sentences.

The cat sat on Ali's lap.

The cat plays with the ball.

The boy has a pet frog.

The frog hops on Sam's bed.

The man sat on his hat.

Time/Phonics Skill IDs IXL TRV • C9A DAY 3

Draw hands on each clock to show the time.

1.
9:00

2.
4:00

3.
11:00

Say the name of each picture. Write the letter of each long vowel sound.

4.
___

5.
___

6.
___

7.
___

 **Let's Play Today** *See page 12.

Many ocean animals, such as crabs and starfish, move in unique ways. Imagine that you are one of these animals. Crawl sideways or move along the ground with arms and legs spread wide.

© Carson Dellosa Education

17

DAY 3

Language Arts & Grammar/Phonics

Add endings to write new words for each base word. (Hint: You may need to add an extra letter before the ending in some words.)

Base Word	Add -ed	Add -ing
8. jump	_____	_____
9. pat	_____	_____
10. open	_____	_____
11. start	_____	_____
12. touch	_____	_____
13. blink	_____	_____

Circle the word that names each picture.

14.

van   vane

15.

mop   mope

16.

slid   slide

Geometry/Phonics

Search for these skill IDs on IXL.com for more practice!

Skill IDs
WVL • LLR

DAY 4

Follow the directions to color each shape.

1.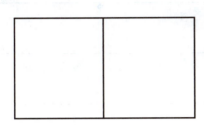

Color one half of the rectangle.

2.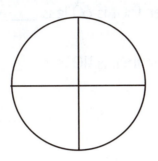

Color one fourth of the circle.

3.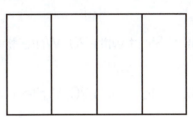

Color two fourths of the rectangle.

Circle the word that names each picture.

4.

can   cane

5.

pan   pane

6.

pin   pine

7.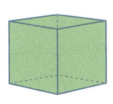

cub   cube

8.

kit   kite

9.

cap   cape

© Carson Dellosa Education

19

Subtraction/Language Arts & Grammar

Follow the directions to solve each problem.

10. Start with 80. Write the number that is 60 less. _____

11. Start with 90. Write the number that is 40 less. _____

12. Start with 20. Write the number that is 10 less. _____

13. Start with 70. Write the number that is 50 less. _____

14. Start with 60. Write the number that is 30 less. _____

15. Start with 50. Write the number that is 10 less. _____

Write the correct ending punctuation mark for each sentence.

16. Do you like carrots _____

17. Are bears fuzzy _____

18. Jan can blow bubbles _____

19. Babies drink milk _____

20. Can you jump rope _____

21. Are clouds white _____

22. That movie was great _____

23. Watch out for that puddle _____

24. The woman is happy _____

25. What is your name _____

Addition & Subtraction/Phonics

 Skill IDs XZB • NZK

DAY 5

Use each fact family to write two addition and two subtraction number sentences.

1.

8 + 5 = 13

☐ + ☐ = ☐

☐ − ☐ = ☐

☐ − ☐ = ☐

2.

☐ + ☐ = ☐

☐ + ☐ = ☐

☐ − ☐ = ☐

☐ − ☐ = ☐

3.

☐ + ☐ = ☐

☐ + ☐ = ☐

☐ − ☐ = ☐

☐ − ☐ = ☐

Say the name of each picture. Write the letter of each short vowel sound.

4.

5.

6.

7.

8.

9.

© Carson Dellosa Education

DAY 5

Addition/Language Arts & Grammar

Write each missing addend.

10.   9
    +[ ]
    ―――
     13

11.   6
    +[ ]
    ―――
     15

12.   9
    +[ ]
    ―――
     18

13.   4
    +[ ]
    ―――
     13

14.   4
    +[ ]
    ―――
     10

15.   7
    +[ ]
    ―――
     16

16.   7
    +[ ]
    ―――
     11

17.   6
    +[ ]
    ―――
     14

Add missing commas to the dates. Use this symbol to add them: ⁁.

18. My grandma was born on August 5 1958.

19. Ali had his third birthday on April 18 2023.

20. On August 11 2011, Mom and Dad got married.

21. Did you know that the house was finished on June 4 2012?

22. If Selena was born on October 23 2007, how old is she now?

Fast Fun Fact

The largest type of frog is the goliath frog. It can grow up to 12 inches (about 30 cm) in length.

22

© Carson Dellosa Education

Place Value/Phonics  DAY 6

Count the tens and ones. Write each number.

1. 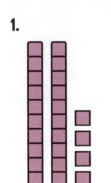 ____

2. 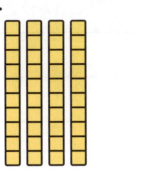 ____

3. 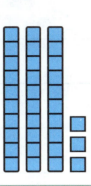 ____

4. 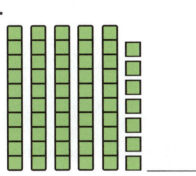 ____

5. 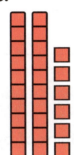 ____

6. 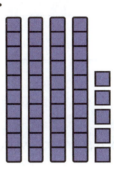 ____

Say the name of each picture. Write the letter of each long vowel sound.

7.  ____

8.  ____

9.  ____

10.  ____

11. 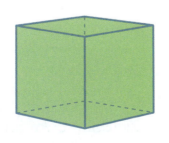 ____

12. 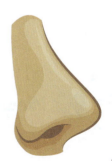 ____

23

Language Arts & Grammar

A base word is a word that has no endings added to it. On the line, write the base word in each word.

13. reading _____

14. angrier _____

15. kicking _____

16. watched _____

17. smoothest _____

18. happily _____

Under the base word, write new words you can think of by adding prefixes and suffixes.

care

_____

_____

_____

_____

_____

Mindful Moment

Make a list of things you can do to calm down. Then, next time you are upset, refer to your list for help.

Problem Solving/Place Value

IXL Skill IDs
YZM • EAN

DAY
7

Solve each problem.

1. Grayson's train has 8 green cars and 7 red cars. How many train cars does Grayson's train have in all?

2. Twelve deer are standing in a field. Four deer run away. How many deer are left in the field?

3. David has 20 spelling words. He misspells 2 words. How many words does he spell correctly?

4. Misha has 13 markers. She finds 6 more markers under her bed. How many markers does Misha have in all?

Write how many tens and ones.

5. 46 = _____ tens _____ ones

6. 19 = _____ ten _____ ones

7. 84 = _____ tens _____ ones

8. 64 = _____ tens _____ ones

Write the number.

9. 4 tens and 0 ones = _____

10. 1 ten and 1 one = _____

11. 9 tens and 3 ones = _____

12. 2 tens and 8 ones = _____

© Carson Dellosa Education

25

DAY 7

Problem Solving/Phonics

Solve each problem.

13. Hattie picked 8 tulips, 6 daffodils, and 3 violets. How many flowers did she pick in all?

14. Henry has 2 sheep, 7 goats, and 9 chickens. How many animals does Henry have?

15. Tariq ate 12 grapes, 3 cherries, and 5 strawberries. How many pieces of fruit did he eat in all?

16. Anya spotted 4 frogs, 4 dragonflies, and 6 turtles at the pond. How many animals did she see in all?

Circle the word that names each picture.

17.

boy
bone
bow

18.

eagle
egg
eye

19.

sun
sand
snake

26 © Carson Dellosa Education

Number Relationships/Writing

Skill ID AMQ — IXL

DAY 8

Circle the number sentences that are true.

1. $7 = 7$

2. $8 - 5 = 3$

3. $7 = 8$

4. $9 - 7 = 3$

5. $4 + 3 = 7$

6. $6 = 4 + 3$

7. $2 + 3 = 5$

8. $2 = 1 + 1$

9. $7 + 4 = 3$

10. $9 = 3 + 6$

11. $5 + 2 = 2 + 5$

12. $4 + 3 = 3 + 4$

Think of three ways to finish this sentence. Write your sentences on the lines.

I liked first grade because . . .

_____

_____

_____

_____

_____

© Carson Dellosa Education

27

Vocabulary/Writing

Circle the word that completes each sentence. Write the word on the line.

13. At night, the sky is _____.

    day   dark   down

14. The _____ came to the party.

    game   sun   girls

15. A rabbit can _____ to the fence.

    hop   hat   boy

16. Andy's dog got _____ in the pond.

    wet   when   hop

Complete the sentences. Ask an adult if you need help.

When I was a baby, I learned to talk. I learned to talk when I was _____ months old. My first words were _____ , _____ , and _____ . If babies could talk even more, they would tell us _____ _____.

Let's Play Today *See page 12.

Pretend that you are rock climbing. Lie on your back and stretch your right arm out in front as far as you can. Now, stretch your left leg toward the sky. Switch arms and legs and slowly "climb the mountain."

Reading Comprehension

Read the story. Then, answer the questions.

Xander woke up slowly. He stretched. Something felt odd. Was it too early to get up? Xander checked his clock. It was almost 8:00, the same time he always got up in the summer. Xander padded over to the window.

The air looked thick and heavy. He could not see the far side of the yard. Xander ran to the back door. He slipped on some shoes. Then, he went outside. Everything was quiet. It felt like a thick gray blanket lay over the yard. He had never seen fog like this before.

1. What words in the story tell how things look, feel, and sound?

   _____
   _____
   _____

2. Where does the story take place? Describe the place.

   _____
   _____
   _____

3. Write what happened first, next, and last in the story.

   _____
   _____
   _____

Circle the letter of the phrase that tells what each poem is about.

4. This is a man who is usually wealthy.
   He might live a long time if he keeps himself healthy.
   His castle's his home, but there's one special thing.
   He can always say, "Dad," when he talks to the king.

   A. a king   B. a president
   C. a doctor   D. a prince

5. I've never seen them, but I've heard them scurry.
   When I open the cupboard door, they leave in a hurry.
   They never say please when they take all of our cheese.
   And they don't like our big, gray cat Murray.

   A. relatives   B. mice
   C. friends   D. cats

Use a small object, such as a paper clip, to measure each item in the list. Write how many of the object you used end to end to measure the items.

I used _____ as a unit of measurement.

a pillow = _____

a windowsill = _____

a shoe = _____

a box of cereal = _____

a notebook = _____

Subtraction/Reading Comprehension

DAY 10

Draw a line from each balloon to its answer.

1. 　2. 　3. 　4.

Draw a line to match each sentence with the correct job.

5. I deliver letters and packages.　　　farmer

6. I help people get well.　　　pilot

7. I grow things to eat.　　　mail carrier

8. I fly airplanes.　　　teacher

9. I work in a school.　　　baker

10. I bake cakes and bread.　　　doctor

DAY 10

Phonics/Spelling

Read each word. Color the space blue if the word has the *long i* sound. Color the space green if the word has the *short i* sound.

bib	fry	tie	light	my	sigh	try	wig
six	bike	sign	pie	guy	by	high	if
fib	gift	pit	dry	bite	miss	fish	lit
chin	sit	hill	time	night	hid	bill	quit
bin	mitt	tin	cry	dime	win	fit	will
pin	fine	lie	sight	why	right	shy	fin
zip	ride	buy	side	hike	kite	nine	did

Underline each misspelled word. Write the word correctly on the line.

11. Ebony backed a cake. _____

12. Libby and I whent to the zoo. _____

13. William has a trane. _____

14. Clean your rom! _____

Fast Fun Fact

Glass takes one million years to decompose. It can be recycled over and over without wearing out!

Addition & Subtraction

IXL Skill IDs: WD2 • Y8Y

DAY 11

Complete each fact family.

1. 2, 3, 5

   2 + 3 = ☐

   3 + ☐ = 5

   5 − 2 = ☐

   ☐ − 3 = 2

2. 2, 7, 9

   7 + 2 = ☐

   ☐ + 7 = 9

   9 − ☐ = 2

   9 − ☐ = 7

3. 3, 5, 8

   5 + 3 = ☐

   ☐ + ☐ = 8

   8 − ☐ = ☐

   ☐ − 3 = ☐

Changing the order of addends in an addition sentence does not change the answer. Complete the sentences below.

4. ||||| + |||||| = |||||| + |||||

     5   +   7   =   _____ + _____

5.   🧦🧦🧦🧦🧦🧦🧦🧦🧦 + 🧦🧦🧦🧦🧦🧦 = 🧦🧦🧦🧦🧦🧦 + 🧦🧦🧦🧦🧦🧦🧦🧦🧦

     9   +   6   =   _____ + _____

6.   ⚽⚽⚽⚽⚽⚽⚽⚽ + ⚽⚽⚽⚽⚽ = ⚽⚽⚽⚽⚽ + ⚽⚽⚽⚽⚽⚽⚽⚽

     8   +   5   =   _____ + _____

Mindful Moment

Share with a friend or family member a time when you were disappointed. Discuss how you changed your mindset.

DAY 11

Search for this skill ID on IXL.com for more practice!

Reading Comprehension

Read the story. Answer the questions.

At the Pond

One warm spring day, some ducklings decided to go to a pond. They wanted to go swim.

"Can we go too?" asked the chicks.

"Chicks can't swim," laughed the ducklings.

"We will run in the tall grass and look for bugs. Please let us go with you," begged the chicks. So, the ducklings and the chicks set off for the pond.

The ducklings swam in the pond. They splashed in the water. The chicks ran in the tall grass. They looked for bugs. The ducklings and the chicks had fun.

After a while, the ducklings and the chicks were tired from playing. They missed their mothers. They missed their nests. It was time to go home.

7. Which sentence tells the main idea of the story?

   A.   Ducklings have fun swimming.

   B.   Chicks and ducklings hatch from eggs.

   C.   The ducklings and the chicks had fun at the pond.

8. Number the story events in order.

   _____ The ducklings swam while the chicks ran in the grass.

   _____ The ducklings wanted to go to the pond.

   _____ The ducklings and the chicks were tired. It was time to go home.

34   © Carson Dellosa Education

Addition/Phonics

Addends on each side of an equal sign can be different as long as they add to the same sum. Write the missing numbers on the lines.

1. 4 + 8 + 2 = _____ + 10

2. 10 + _____ = 5 + 5 + 9

3. 6 + 6 + 4 = _____ + 6

4. 3 + 7 + _____ = 10 + 1

5. 9 + _____ + 8 = 10 + 8

6. 10 + 0 + 2 = 10 + _____

Say the name of each picture. Write the letters of the beginning blend in each word.

7.
_____ _____

8.
_____ _____

9.
_____ _____

10.
_____ _____

11.
_____ _____

12.
_____ _____

Addition & Subtraction/Language Arts & Grammar

On the pie to the left, write the number that is 10 less than the number shown. On the pie to the right, write the number that is 10 more.

13.

14.

15.

16.

Unscramble each sentence. Write the words in the correct order.

17. swim like Ducks to.

   _____

18. we sandbox Can play in the?

   _____

19. nests birds in trees Some make.

   _____

20. fun today Are having you?

   _____

Language Arts & Grammar/Phonics

Each sentence is missing at least one capital letter. Make three small lines under letters that should be capitals like this: f.

1. Myles kicked the ball to stella.

2. Coach rodrigo asked me to go first.

3. kerry scored four home runs in august!

4. Antonio's soccer game is on july 8th.

Say the name of each picture. Circle the pictures that have the *long a* sound, as in *tape*.

© Carson Dellosa Education

DAY 13

Skill IDs
WNY • 8QD

Language Arts & Grammar/Phonics

Rewrite each set of words below to make it show ownership.

5.

   the muffin belonging to Peter ___Peter's muffin_____

6.

   the kite belonging to Kate _____

7.

   the hat belonging to Hasaan _____

8.

   the soccer ball belonging to Sammy _____

Read each word. Color the heart pink if the word has a *long u* sound. Color the heart red if the word has a *short u* sound.

9.
10.
11.
12.

Let's Play Today *See page 12.

Play a game of "Simon Says . . . Stretch!" For each command, say a body part to stretch.

38 © Carson Dellosa Education

Addition & Subtraction/Language Arts & Grammar

Complete each fact family.

1.

    4 + 5 = ☐

    5 + 4 = ☐

    9 - 5 = ☐

    9 - 4 = ☐

2.

    6 + ☐ = 8

    2 + ☐ = ☐

    8 - ☐ = 2

    8 - ☐ = ☐

3.

    ☐ + ☐ = ☐

    ☐ + ☐ = ☐

    ☐ + ☐ = ☐

    ☐ + ☐ = ☐

Read each noun. Write it in the correct column.

Olivia	Dr. Yang	cousin
hippo	holiday	store
Greenlawn Library	Thanksgiving	

Common Nouns

_____

_____

_____

Proper Nouns

_____

_____

_____

Reading Comprehension/Language Arts & Grammar

Circle the letter of the sentence that describes each picture.

4. A. Dez walked up the stairs.

   B. Dez walked down the stairs.

   C. Dez sat on the stairs.

5. A. Sohkna and Justin play baseball.

   B. Sohkna and Justin take karate.

   C. Sohkna and Justin study math.

Write a word from the box to replace each word or words in bold type.

| her | his | their |

6. **Harry's** birthday = _____ birthday

7. **the kids'** puppies = _____ puppies

8. **Hanna's** life jacket = _____ life jacket

Problem Solving

Solve each problem.

1. Iman has 9 baseballs. He finds 3 more. How many baseballs does he have in all?

2. A farmer has 12 apples. He makes a pie with 5 of them. How many apples does he have left?

3. Beth bakes 12 cookies. Her dad bakes 6 more. How many cookies did they bake in all?

4. There are 10 kittens in the basket. Four kittens hop out of the basket. How many kittens are still in the basket?

5. Toru has 16 trading cards. He gives his friend 3 cards. How many cards does Toru have left?

6. Gina found 8 seashells. Gabe found 6 seashells. How many seashells did they find altogether?

Search for this skill ID on IXL.com for more practice!

Reading Comprehension

Read the story. Answer the questions.

A Place for Little Frog

Little Frog hopped out of the pond. "Where are you going, Little Frog?" asked the other frogs.

"I'm tired of living in this pond with so many frogs," he said. "I need more space." So Little Frog hopped away.

Soon, he met a bee. When he told the bee his story, the bee buzzed, "You cannot live with me. You would get stuck in my honey."

Next, Little Frog met a dog. The dog barked and chased Little Frog away. "Living with a dog is not the place for me," said Little Frog.

Little Frog hopped and hopped all the way back to his pond. The other frogs were happy to see him. They moved over to make room for him. Little Frog settled in, smiled, and said, "Now, this is the place for me."

7. Which sentence tells the main idea of the story?

  A. A hive is no place for a frog.

  B. Dogs do not like frogs.

  C. Little Frog found out that his own home is best.

8. Number the story events in order.

  _____ Little Frog hopped all the way back to his pond.

  _____ Little Frog hopped out of the pond.

  _____ A dog chased Little Frog away.

Fast Fun Fact

Millions of trees have been accidentally planted by squirrels because they have forgotten where they've hidden their nuts!

Language Arts & Grammar

Write a letter to tell what kind of sentence each one is.

S = Statement   Q = Question   C = Command   E = Exclamation

1. _____ What time does the game start?
2. _____ Zane just hit a home run!
3. _____ Pass me the bug spray.
4. _____ Oliver is on first base.
5. _____ Destiny is the fastest runner on our team.

Choose the conjuction that completes each sentence. Write it on the line.

6. Drew _____ Mom went to the farmers' market.
   (and, but)

7. Do you like corn _____ carrots better?
   (or, but)

8. The market had eggs, _____ we will have omelets today.
   (or, so)

9. Drew loves peas, _____ all the farmers were sold out.
   (but, because)

DAY 16

Reading Comprehension/Phonics

Fill in the circle beside the sentence that best describes each picture.

10.

○ The bees are on the flower.
○ The bees are under the flower.
○ The bees are around the hive.

11.

○ The bird is on the bowl.
○ The bird loves to sing.
○ The bird never sings.

Say the name of each picture. Write the number of syllables in each name.

12.

_____

13.

_____

14.

_____

15.

_____

Mindful Moment

Discuss with an adult what you think is the best way to handle a change in plans.

© Carson Dellosa Education

Language Arts & Grammar/Phonics

Add the word parts. Write the new word on the line.

1. melt + ed = _____

2. sweet + er = _____

3. un + tie = _____

4. fear + ful = _____

5. re + read = _____

6. pre + heat = _____

Say the name of each picture. Write the letter of each vowel sound.

7.  c _____ ke	8.  b _____ x	9.  d _____ ck
10.  l _____ mp	11.  m _____ lk	12.  m _____ ce

© Carson Dellosa Education

45

DAY 17

Search for these skill IDs on IXL.com for more practice!

Geometry/Phonics

Write the word or phrase that tells where each shape is. The shapes are *on top of*, *under*, or *next to* other shapes.

13. The triangle is _____ the square.

14. The circle is _____ the square.

15. The square is _____ the triangle.

Draw a line to match each butterfly to the flower that has the same long vowel sound.

great

ā

break

peach

beat

ē

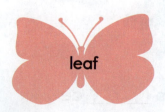
leaf

steak

Place Value/Writing

Write how many tens and ones are in each number.

1. 26 = _____ tens _____ ones
2. 41 = _____ tens _____ one
3. 45 = _____ tens _____ ones
4. 84 = _____ tens _____ ones
5. 65 = _____ tens _____ ones
6. 72 = _____ tens _____ ones
7. 17 = _____ ten _____ ones
8. 39 = _____ tens _____ ones
9. 50 = _____ tens _____ ones
10. 51 = _____ tens _____ one
11. 97 = _____ tens _____ ones
12. 100 = _____ tens _____ ones

Write a paragraph for a younger brother or sister, cousin, or friend. Explain how to do something step-by-step. You could explain how to feed a pet, make a sandwich, or plant a seed.

_____

_____

_____

_____

_____

_____

_____

_____

DAY 18

Skill ID 8YT

Reading Comprehension/Writing

Number the sentences in the order that the events happened.

13. _____ The sun came out. It became a pretty day.

14. _____ It started to rain.

15. _____ Hannah put her umbrella away.

16. _____ Hannah used her umbrella.

17. _____ The clouds came, and the sky was dark.

What do you think the perfect tree house would look like? Describe it and draw a picture of it.

_____

_____

_____

_____

_____

_____

_____

Let's Play Today *See page 12.

Imagine you are a rubber band. Stretch and release your body. Do this slowly 10 times.

Number Relationships/Geometry

Write > or < to compare each set of numbers.

1. 11 ◯ 13
2. 91 ◯ 87
3. 55 ◯ 75
4. 46 ◯ 29
5. 39 ◯ 27
6. 78 ◯ 33
7. 24 ◯ 19
8. 73 ◯ 85
9. 48 ◯ 100
10. 14 ◯ 21
11. 62 ◯ 56
12. 94 ◯ 78
13. 18 ◯ 47
14. 54 ◯ 62
15. 50 ◯ 44

Use the directions to draw each shape.

16. Draw a shape that has no sides and no corners.

17. Draw a shape that has three sides and three corners.

18. Draw a shape that has four sides of equal length.

19. Draw a shape that has four sides and four corners. Opposite sides are equal in length.

DAY 19

Reading Comprehension/Writing

Solve each riddle.

20. I am tiny. I have three body parts and six legs. I can be a real pest at picnics.

    I am an _____.

21. I was just born. My parents feed me. I cry and sleep, but I cannot walk.

    I am a _____.

22. I am made of metal and can be small. I can lock doors and unlock them, too.

    I am a _____.

23. I have four legs. I like to play. I bark.

    I am a _____.

Write your own riddle. Ask a friend or family member to solve it.

_____
_____
_____
_____
_____

Time/Phonics

Skill IDs 7N3 • 2FQ

DAY 20

Write the correct time for each clock.

1.

_____:_____

2.

_____:_____

3.

_____:_____

Say the name of each picture. Circle the letters that make each beginning sound.

4.

ch   wh   sh

5.

ch   wh   sh

6.

ch   wh   sh

 **Fast Fun Fact**

A person consumes one-tenth of a calorie every time they lick a stamp.

© Carson Dellosa Education

DAY 20

Measurement/Reading Comprehension

Write **1, 2,** or **3** on each line to order the objects from shortest to longest.

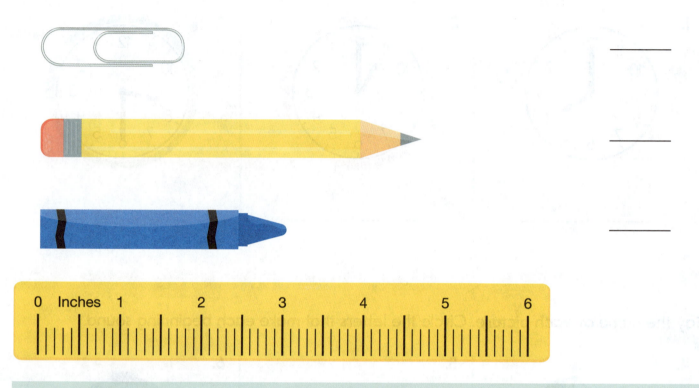

Write the letter of the title next to the story it matches.

TITLES
A. The Turtle Dream   **B.** The Sleepover   **C.** A Wish Before Bed

7. _____ Jenna made a wish every night before going to sleep. She would look in the sky for the brightest star. Then, she would close her eyes and make a wish.

8. _____ Malia fell asleep in the car on the way to the beach. She dreamed that she was a flying turtle. She flew all around the beach. No one could catch her.

9. _____ Kendra had her friend Leslie sleep over. They watched a movie and ate popcorn. They made a tent out of blankets. They slept in the tent.

52 © Carson Dellosa Education

Science Experiment

Upside-Down Water

Can you turn a cup of water upside down without spilling it?

Materials:
- index card
- clear plastic cup
- water

Procedure:
1. Do this experiment over a sink.
2. Fill the cup halfway with water.
3. Put the index card on top of the cup. Put your hand over the card. Turn the cup upside down over the sink.
4. Wait two seconds. Then, move your hand away.

What's This All About?
When you flip the cup, the air outside of the cup pushes on the card. The air pushes harder than the water inside the cup. If you wiggle the card before you move your hand, the water molecules on the card and the rim of the cup will stick together. Then, air cannot get in and equalize the pressure.

More Fun Ideas to Try:
- Use different amounts of water in the cup.
- Try different types of paper. You can use construction paper, wrapping paper, or notebook paper.
- Find out how long you can hold the cup upside down before water starts to spill out.
- Try plastic cups of different sizes and shapes.
- Write a letter or an e-mail to a friend or relative. Tell about the experiment you did. Explain how it works and what your results were.

BONUS

Science Experiment

The Flying Sheet of Paper

How do planes fly?

Materials:
- sheet of paper

Procedure:
1. Hold a sheet of paper just under your bottom lip. Curve the top of the paper slightly. What do you think will happen to the paper if you blow down and across the top of it? Do you think it will hit you in the chest, stay where it is, or bounce up and hit you in the nose?
2. Write your prediction on a separate sheet of paper.
3. Blow down and across the top of the paper.

What's This All About?
By blowing down and across the top of the paper, you cause air molecules to move faster across the paper rather than moving around as they normally do. Faster moving air molecules lower the air pressure on the top of the paper. Higher air pressure under the paper pushes the paper up. For an airplane to fly, the air pressure must be lower on top of the wings than under them. The higher air pressure under the wings pushes the airplane up.

More Fun Ideas to Try:
The next time you take a shower, notice what the shower curtain does. Does it balloon away, or does it move closer to you? Do you know why?

Social Studies Activity

Search for this skill ID on IXL.com for more practice! Skill ID R2U BONUS

My Own Map

Maps have many uses. A pilot uses maps to find the right flight paths. A hiker uses a map to find their way on a trail. A traveler uses a map to get around a new town.

Work on your mapmaking skills by drawing a map of a path that is in or around your home. You will need a sheet of paper and a pencil. Be as accurate as possible. If you are drawing a path from your room to the refrigerator, include hallways, stairways, rooms, and furniture that you pass as you walk.

Try your map when it is finished. Follow the path as you drew it. Make changes if needed. Then, have a friend or family member try your map. Ask them to use the map to follow the path to the end. Have a surprise treat waiting for them, such as a snack to share.

© Carson Dellosa Education

55

BONUS

Social Studies Activity

The State of Things

It is important to learn about where you live. Your state or province might be the home of the first candy factory or the only state or province with a professional trampoline team. With an adult, search the Internet to find interesting information about where you live. Share the fun facts with family and friends. Below are some search terms to get you started:

- facts about [your state or province name]
- government site for kids
- local library website

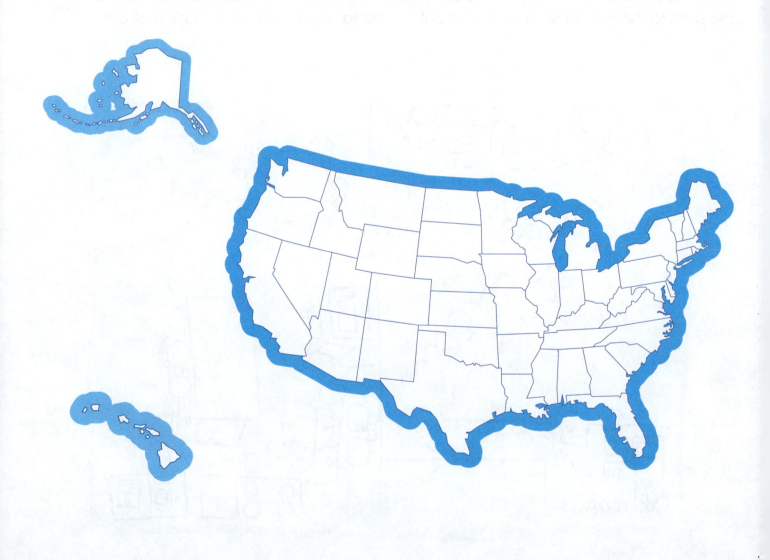

Social Studies Activity

International Cuisine*

You can learn a lot about other countries by making and eating some of their native dishes. Think of a country you would like to know more about. Find out what foods the people from that country eat. For example, if you want to learn about France, go to the library with an adult and check out French cookbooks or books about French food. Or, search the Internet with an adult to find recipes for French dishes.

Choose a simple recipe with ingredients that you and an adult can buy at your local grocery store. Whether you make soup, salad, or another treat from the country, you will "taste" a bit of the country when you eat the food. Get your family involved. Invite each family member to choose a country and enjoy trying different foods from places around the world.

*See page 2.

© Carson Dellosa Education

57

SECTION 2

Monthly Goals

Think of three goals to set for yourself this month. For example, you may want to spend more time reading with your family. Have an adult help you write your goals on the lines.

Place a sticker next to each of your goals that you complete. Feel proud that you have met your goals!

1. _____ [PLACE STICKER HERE]

2. _____ [PLACE STICKER HERE]

3. _____ [PLACE STICKER HERE]

Word List

The following words are used in this section. Read each word aloud with an adult. When you see a word from this list on a page, circle it with your favorite color of crayon.

adjective   passage

attempts   strength

describe   struggle

difference   tally

habitat   vanish

Introduction to Strength

This section includes Let's Play Today and Mindful Moments activities that focus on strength. These activities are designed to help your child spend less time on a screen and more time developing healthy emotional and physical habits. If your child has limited mobility, feel free to modify any suggested activity or choose a different one from the list on the following page.

Let's Play Today

Like flexibility, strength is necessary for a child to be healthy. Children might think being strong means lifting an enormous amount of weight. However, strength is more than the ability to pick up heavy barbells. Explain that strength is built over time and point out to your child how much stronger they have become since they were a toddler. At that time, they could walk down the sidewalk. Now they can run across a baseball field.

Everyday activities, fun exercises, and enjoyable games provide opportunities for children to gain strength. Your child could take a walk, do a classic exercise such as push ups, or play a game of basketball or tag. All of these build physical strength.

Help your child set realistic, achievable goals to improve their physical strength based on their ability and the activities they enjoy. Over the summer months, offer encouragement and praise as your child accomplishes their strength goals.

Mindful Moments

Having strength of character on the inside is just as important as having physical strength on the outside. Explain to your child that being a strong person on the inside can be shown by being honest, facing a fear, helping others, standing up for someone who needs a friend, or choosing to do the right thing when presented with a difficult situation. Talk about real-life examples with your child. When have they had inner strength to handle a situation? Look for moments to acknowledge when your child has demonstrated strength of character so that they can see their positive growth on the inside as well as on the outside.

Engaging Online Practice

Bring learning to life with fun, interactive activities on IXL! Look for the Skill ID box and type the 3-digit code into the search bar on IXL.com or the IXL mobile app. Ten questions per day are free!

Skill IDs
5UN • D9K

SECTION 2

Let's Play Today

Get your child up and moving with these Let's Play Today activities. Section 2 focuses on strength. Strengthening exercises make our bones and muscles stronger. Strong bones and muscles help prevent injury and speed up recovery from injury. Use this list in addition to or as a replacement for any Let's Play Today suggestions on the activity pages. This list was developed to be inclusive of a variety of abilities. Choose the ones that suit your child the best! Make modifications as needed. These activities may require adult supervision. See page 2 for full caution information.

Lava Pit:

Hop from pillow to pillow on an imaginary bed of lava. Start with just 3-4 pillows and repeat it two times. Over time, gradually add pillows to work up to a longer, more complex path of pillows. Repeat hopping on the longer path 10 times.

Frog Hops:

Crouch down with your hands on the floor in a frog-like position. Hop forward like a frog 3-4 times. Over time, gradually increase the number of hops until you get to 15.

Shadow Fun:

Go outside on a sunny day and make sure you can see your shadow. If you are by yourself, practice shadow boxing. Bend your arms at the elbows and bring your hands back to your body. Make a fist with each hand. Extend one arm at a time to mimic a boxing motion. If someone is outside with you, trace each other's shadow with chalk. Hold a pose that works your muscles, such as standing on one leg or flexing your arms.

Balloon Back-and-Forth:

Either seated or standing, hit a balloon up into the air to another person. That person will hit it back to you. Keep track of how many times you can hit it to each other without it touching the ground. Try to increase your score.

Swim Like a Fish:

Wearing a life jacket in the shallow end of a pool, try swimming like a fish! Use flippers to help. See how many different ways to swim you can come up with. For example, swim like you have a fish tail, swim without using your arms, swim with flippers on your hands, or roll around.

Counting/Language Arts & Grammar

Skill IDs
ET8 • 7FP

DAY 1

Skip count. Write the missing numbers.

1.  60 ___ 70 75 ___ ___ 90 95

2.  320 ___ 340 350 ___ 370 ___ 390

3. 300 400 ___ ___ 700 ___ 900 1,000

Write adjectives to describe each object.

4. teddy bear

_____

_____

_____

_____

5. gift

_____

_____

_____

_____

© Carson Dellosa Education

61

DAY 1 — Language Arts & Grammar/Addition

Unscramble each sentence. Write the words in the correct order.

6. sun shine today will The.

   _____

7. mile today I a walked.

   _____

8. fence We painted our.

   _____

9. me knit will She something for.

   _____

Follow the directions to solve each problem.

10. Start with 54. Write the number that is 100 more. _____

11. Start with 80. Write the number that is 10 more. _____

12. Start with 22. Write the number that is 100 more. _____

13. Start with 65. Write the number that is 10 more. _____

Mindful Moment

Discuss with an adult the best time and way to ask for something.

62 © Carson Dellosa Education

Number Relationships/Phonics

Search for these skill IDs on IXL.com for more practice!

DAY 2

Circle the greater number in each set.

1. 17 or 71
2. 91 or 19
3. 67 or 72
4. 34 or 30
5. 26 or 41
6. 29 or 40
7. 90 or 99
8. 79 or 80
9. 44 or 54

Circle the word that names each picture. Write the word on the line.

10.    glove / glass

11.    frog / flag

12.    clown / clock

13.    bow / bowl

DAY 2

Reading Comprehension / Language Arts & Grammar

Read each paragraph. Circle the letter of the best title.

14. Carlos is at bat. He hits the ball. He runs to first base and then to second base. Will Carlos make it all the way to home plate?

   A. Running

   B. Carlos Like to Play

   C. Carlos's Baseball Game

15. Madison put on sunscreen and sunglasses. Then, she found her favorite green hat. Madison was ready to go outside.

   A. A Rainy Day

   B. Ready to Go Out in the Sun

   C. Madison Likes to Play

Draw a line to match each contraction to its word pair.

16. didn't		it is
17. it's		we will
18. we're		did not
19. you've		we are
20. don't		is not
21. we'll		you have
22. isn't		do not

Problem Solving

 Skill ID 6X3

DAY 3

Solve each problem. Use the bank of objects and prices.

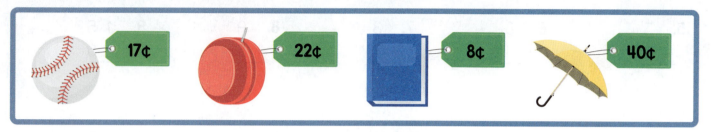

1. Lori bought an umbrella and a book. How much money did she spend?

2. Henry bought a yo-yo and an umbrella. How much money did he spend?

3. Maria bought a baseball and a yo-yo. How much money did she spend?

4. Alejandro bought a baseball and a book. How much money did he spend?

Write two of your own word problems. Use the same bank of objects or draw your own.

_____

_____

_____

_____

DAY 3

Addition & Subtraction/Phonics

Solve each problem.

5. 5
   +7

6. 8
   +4

7. 3
   +7

8. 9
   +5

9. 1 5
   +   5

10. 1 2
   −   8

11. 9
   − 4

12. 1 1
   −   7

13. 8
   − 8

14. 1 0
   −   2

Write the word that matches each set of clues.

15. It begins like stuck.
    It rhymes with late. ____state____

16. It begins like rip.
    It rhymes with cake. _____

17. It begins like tiger.
    It rhymes with bag. _____

18. It begins like cat.
    It rhymes with ball. _____

19. It begins like gum.
    It rhymes with late. _____

Let's Play Today *See page 60.

Take 10 baby steps. Then, take 10 giant steps.

Vocabulary/Numbers

DAY 4

Similar words can have different shades of meaning. Underline the word that best completes each sentence.

1. Jamilla carefully (sipped, gulped) the hot tea.
2. Dana (tapped, pounded) on her parents' door when she heard the fire alarm.
3. Lex felt (nervous, terrified) when he realized he had forgotten his permission slip.
4. Dad was (tired, exhausted) after driving all through the night to get home.

How many are in each group? Write the number on the line. Then, circle *odd* or *even*.

5. _____ odd   even

6. _____ odd   even

7. _____ odd   even

8. _____ odd   even

Phonics/Spelling

Say each word in the box. Listen for the long vowel sound. Write the word under the correct heading.

bugle	apron	bedtime	Monday	human
eagle	rider	argue	flavor	hello
frozen	ocean	unkind	season	fever

Long a

_____

_____

_____

Long e

_____

_____

_____

Long i

_____

_____

_____

Long o

_____

_____

_____

Long u

_____

_____

_____

Underline the misspelled word in each sentence. Then, write each word correctly on the line.

9. What may I help yu with? _____

10. Please giv him a fork. _____

11. You can sti on the chair. _____

12. Will you miks the paint? _____

68

Graphing  Skill ID 6KD

DAY 5

Which flavor of ice cream is the most popular with your friends and family? Ask each person to choose a favorite ice-cream flavor from the list. Make a tally mark beside each answer given.

vanilla _____ butter pecan _____

chocolate _____ cookies 'n' cream _____

strawberry _____ other _____

Count the tally marks beside each flavor. Graph your results.

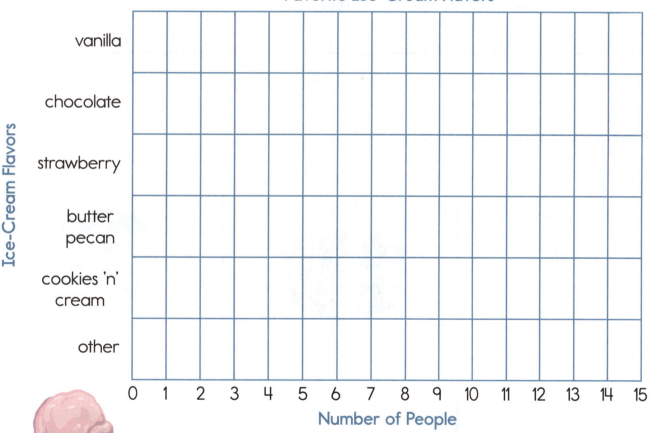

© Carson Dellosa Education

69

DAY 5

Reading Comprehension/Phonics

Read the story. Answer the questions.

    Olivia lives on a farm. She wakes up early to do chores. Olivia feeds all the horses and chickens. She also collects the eggs. Sometimes, she helps her dad milk the cows. Her favorite thing to do in the morning is eat breakfast.

1. Where does Olivia live? _____

2. Why does she wake up early? _____

3. Write one chore that Olivia does. _____

4. What is her favorite thing to do in the morning? _____

_____

Circle the word that names each picture.

5.

coin

coyn

6.

boyl

boil

7.

toi

toy

Fast Fun Fact

Donkeys can see all four of their feet at the same time.

70   © Carson Dellosa Education

Addition/Problem Solving

Search for this skill ID on IXL.com for more practice!  Skill ID Z7S

DAY 6

Add to find each sum.

1. 2
    5
    + 2
    ___

2. 1
    1
    + 1
    ___

3. 4
    4
    + 4
    ___

4. 5
    5
    + 5
    ___

5. 2
    3
    + 2
    ___

6. 4
    3
    + 0
    ___

7. 5
    4
    + 5
    ___

8. 3
    3
    + 3
    ___

9. 4
    6
    + 5
    ___

10. 6
    4
    + 2
    ___

11. 7
    0
    + 7
    ___

12. 1 0
    1 0
    + 1 0
    _____

Solve each problem.

13. Bev had 5 blue beds, 7 red beads, and 3 yellow beads. How many beads does she have in all?

14. On the table are 6 forks, 9 spoons, and 3 knives. How many utensils are there in all?

© Carson Dellosa Education

71

Subtraction/Spelling

Draw lines to connect the subtraction facts that have the same difference.

15.
5 – 3   5 – 1
8 – 3   9 – 8
8 – 4   7 – 2
5 – 4   6 – 4

16.
8 – 7   10 – 4
3 – 1   4 – 3
8 – 2   5 – 3
9 – 5   7 – 3

17.
10 – 5   13 – 10
12 – 6   7 – 1
2 – 0   9 – 4
9 – 6   4 – 2

18.
5 – 5   14 – 7
12 – 9   8 – 5
11 – 4   8 – 8
12 – 8   5 – 1

Unscramble each word. Spell each word correctly on the line to complete each sentence.

19. Juan had a _____ for _____ mother.
     igft   ihs

20. The _____ has a _____ tire.
        acr   tfla

21. A butterfly _____ on _____ flower.
                 ats   hte

22. My _____ works at the _____ .
        add   tsoer

 **Mindful Moment**

Discuss with an adult what you think are the most important qualities of a good friend.

Reading Comprehension/Problem Solving

DAY 7

Read each paragraph. Underline the sentence that states the main idea.

1. Sidney's umbrella is old. The color is faded. It doesn't keep the rain off her.

2. Tabby is a farm cat. He is tan and white. Tabby helps the farmer by catching mice in the barn. He sleeps on soft hay.

3. Big, gray clouds are in the sky. The wind is blowing, and it is getting colder. I think it will snow.

Solve each problem.

4. Amina has three shelves. One is 14 inches tall, one is 18 inches tall, and one is 21 inches tall. If she stacks all three of them, how tall will her shelves be?

5. On Friday, the high temperature was 86°. It dropped 20° by midnight. What was the temperature at midnight?

6. The first time Dylan measured his sunflower, it was 34 inches tall. The next time, it had grown another 55 inches. How tall was Dylan's sunflower?

7. Mr. Washington mailed 3 packages. The first was 6 pounds, the second was 11 pounds, and the third was 14 pounds. How much did his packages weigh in all?

DAY 7

Geometry/Phonics

Will the figures stack flat on top of each other? Circle *yes* or *no*.

8.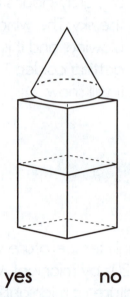

yes   no

9.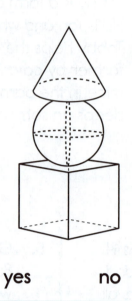

yes   no

10.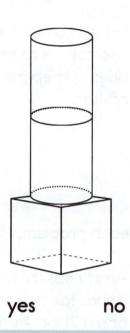

yes   no

Read each word. Write *e* if the *y* makes the *long e* sound, as in *story*. Write *i* if the *y* makes the *long i* sound, as in *sky*.

11.
baby

12.
fly

13.
windy

14.
bunny

15.
shy

16.
family

17.
buy

18.
happy

19.
cry

20.
my

21.
funny

22.
silly

Vocabulary/Phonics

DAY 8

Circle the word in each row that does not belong.

1. bean   carrot   book   lettuce   peas

2. train   jet   leg   car   boat

3. cat   orange   green   blue   red

4. lake   ocean   pond   chair   river

5. bear   apple   lion   wolf   tiger

6. Jane   Kathy   Tom   Jill   Anna

Write *oi* or *oy* to complete each word. Write the word on the line.

7. b ___ ___ _____

8. ___ ___ l _____

9. s ___ ___ l _____

10. v ___ ___ ce _____

 **Let's Play Today** *See page 60.
Do 10 shoulder shrugs and 10 squats.

© Carson Dellosa Education   75

Reading Comprehension

Read the story. Answer the questions.

Flying High

Ben is a baby bald eagle. He is learning to fly. It has been a **struggle** for Ben. He has been practicing for days, but he is not improving.

Getting up in the air is easy. Flying over fields is no problem. But, Ben has trouble flying around things. He does not do well when he **attempts** to land in a certain spot. Perhaps he should sign up for flying lessons to improve his flying skills.

11. The word *struggle* means:
    A. something that is not easy
    B. a boat
    C. a broken wing

12. The word *attempts* means:
    A. sings
    B. tries
    C. waits

13. Learning to fly is hard for Ben. How does he handle it?

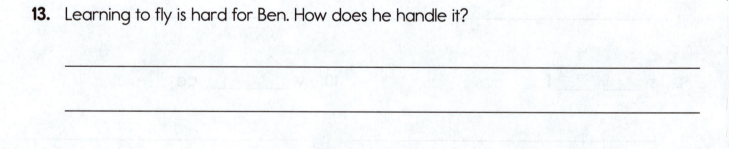

Language Arts & Grammar/Writing

Write the correct verb to complete each sentence.

1. Amelia _____ a song.
   sing   sang

2. Did the bell _____ yet?
   ring   rang

3. The grass _____ green.
   is   are

4. She _____ a race.
   run   ran

5. Mom will _____ a short trip.
   took   take

6. Uncle Chris _____ a new scooter.
   has   have

If you could plant a garden, what would you plant and why?

_____

_____

_____

_____

_____

_____

© Carson Dellosa Education

DAY 9

Problem Solving/Spelling

Solve each problem.

7. Cara spent 18¢. Danielle spent 10¢. How much did they spend altogether?

8. Pilar has 10 stamps. Edward has 15 stamps. How many stamps do they have altogether?

9. Nelan has 16 fish. Jay has 12 fish. How many fish do they have in all?

10. Emily has 13 balloons. Jessi has 10 balloons. How many balloons do they have in all?

Write words to fill in the blanks.

Singular (One)	Plural (More Than One)
child	
mouse	
	feet
man	
	teeth
	people

78

Addition/Phonics

Add to find each sum. Draw a line to match each dog with the correct ball.

1. 3 2
   + 2 1

4. 4 4
   + 1 3

79

53

2. 7 3
   + 2 4

50

57

5. 5 2
   + 2 6

3. 2 0
   + 3 0

97

78

6. 6 1
   + 1 8

Say the name of each picture. Circle the letters that make each ending sound.

7.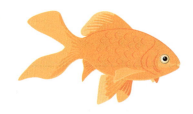

th   sh   ch

8.

th   sh   ch

9.

th   sh   ch

© Carson Dellosa Education

79

DAY 10

Skill IDs: SSL • RW7

Counting/Language Arts & Grammar

Complete each number line.

10. Count by twos.

2   4   6   ___   ___   ___

11. Count by fours.

4   ___   12   ___   ___   ___

12. Count by fives.

5   ___   15   ___   ___   30

Write a contraction from the word bank that means the same thing as each word pair.

| we're | it's | you'll | I'm | she'll | they've |

13. it is _____   14. they have _____

15. we are _____   16. I am _____

17. you will _____   18. she will _____

Fast Fun Fact

A sneeze can travel out of a person's mouth and nose at more than 100 miles (160 km) per hour.

80 © Carson Dellosa Education

Geometry/Writing

Draw lines to divide each rectangle into rows and columns. Then, count the number of small rectangles you made. Write your answer on the line.

1. 3 rows
   4 columns

   How many rectangles? _____

2. 4 rows
   5 columns

   How many rectangles? _____

Have you ever helped someone without the person knowing? How did it make you feel?

_____
_____
_____
_____
_____

81

DAY 11

Search for this skill ID on IXL.com for more practice!

Spelling/Language Arts & Grammar

Rearrange the letters in the phrase to make new words. Write the words on the lines.

camping trip

_____

_____

_____

Draw a line to divide each compound word into two words. Write the words on the line.

3. goldfish
_____

4. popcorn
_____

5. daytime
_____

6. doghouse
_____

7. spaceship
_____

8. railroad
_____

9. blueberry
_____

10. sailboat
_____

11. grapefruit
_____

12. cupcake
_____

13. newspaper
_____

14. sometime
_____

Mindful Moment

Gather your outgrown, gently used toys and books and give them to a local charity.

82 © Carson Dellosa Education

Subtraction/Time Skill IDs PV5 • K7F DAY 12

Subtract to find each difference.

1. 10 − 2
2. 10 − 9
3. 10 − 7
4. 10 − 8
5. 10 − 6

6. 10 − 3
7. 11 − 9
8. 11 − 7
9. 11 − 8
10. 11 − 4

11. 11 − 3
12. 12 − 2
13. 12 − 9
14. 12 − 8
15. 12 − 7

Write the time shown on each clock.

16.
___:___

17.
___:___

18.
___:___

19.
___:___

20.
___:___

21.
___:___

© Carson Dellosa Education

DAY 12

Skill IDs K72 • ZWW

Reading Comprehension/Language Arts & Grammar

Number the sentences in the order that the events happened.

_____ Jenny made a chocolate cake for her friend.

_____ Jenny put blue frosting on the cake.

_____ Jenny put sprinkles on the cake.

_____ Jenny went to the store and bought a box of cake mix.

Draw and color a picture of the cake that Jenny made.

A noun followed by 's shows ownership. One noun in each sentence is missing an apostrophe. Add it like this: Charlie's kitty.

22. We stayed up late at Jonahs sleepover.

23. The cats fur is very soft.

24. Dantes cousin lives in Florida.

25. The maple trees leaves are changing color.

84 © Carson Dellosa Education

Place Value

Choose the crayon whose number matches each description. Use the color listed to color the crayon.

1.
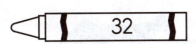
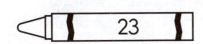

2 tens and 3 ones
blue

2.
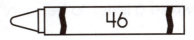
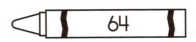

4 tens and 6 ones
green

3.
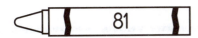
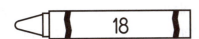

1 ten and 8 ones
purple

4.
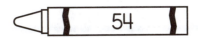
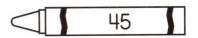

5 tens and 4 ones
orange

5.
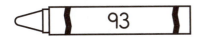
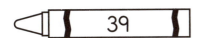

3 tens and 9 ones
black

6.
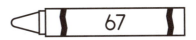
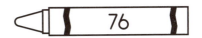

6 tens and 7 ones
brown

 **Let's Play Today** *See page 60.

Lift and lower empty water bottles above your head. Then, fill the bottles with water. Lift and lower 10 times. Which took more strength to lift?

© Carson Dellosa Education

85

Read each sentence and circle each noun. A noun can be a person, place, or thing.

7. The boy took off his muddy shoes.

8. She wrote a letter to her aunt.

9. Did you have a sandwich?

10. We saw a movie about butterflies.

11. My little sister has a shiny ring.

Write the months of the year in order.

October	March	February	April
December	July	November	June
August	May	January	September

_____ _____

_____ _____

_____ _____

_____ _____

_____ _____

_____ _____

Numbers/Phonics

Circle the odd numbers in each row.

1. 2   5   7   3   9   4   6   11 14
2. 1   10 6   7   12 13 15 2   17
3. 5   11 9   13 14 17 19 3   8

Circle the even numbers in each row.

4. 6   9   2   11 4   7   3   8   12
5. 13 8   10 6   12 16 9   5   19
6. 14 16 9   11 12 18 7   4   8

Read each word. Then, find a word in the box that has the same long-vowel spelling. Write it on the line.

| pie | boat | sweet | throw | play | beach |

7. green _____

8. cream _____

9. coat _____

10. lie _____

11. crow _____

12. may _____

Spelling/Writing

Write the correct word to complete each sentence.

13. A dime is a _____ .
    coin   coyn

14. I want to buy my friend a new _____ .
    toi   toy

15. My cat has one white _____ .
    paw   pau

16. Dan has two sons and one _____ .
    daughter   dawter

Invent and design a new kind of juice box. Draw your design below. Describe your new juice box on a separate sheet of paper.

Reading Comprehension

Read the passage. Answer the questions.

Black-Footed Ferrets

Years ago, many black-footed ferrets lived in the American West. They were wild and free. Their **habitat** was destroyed by humans.

The ferrets began to **vanish**. Almost all of them died. Scientists worked to save the ferrets' lives. Now, the number of ferrets has increased.

1. Where did the black-footed ferrets live?

   _____

2. Who worked to save the ferrets? _____

   _____

3. What happened after scientists started to help the ferrets?

   _____

   _____

4. The word *habitat* means:
   A. a costume worn by ferrets
   B. a pattern of behavior
   C. a place where something lives

5. The word *vanish* means:
   A. to be born
   B. to disappear
   C. to clean one's home

Fast Fun Fact

Although a polar bear appears white, its skin is black. Its fur is made up of many colorless, hollow tubes.

DAY 15

IXL Skill IDs YKL • LDW

Addition & Subtraction/Language Arts & Grammar

Write the correct numbers to get the answer in each box.

6. $4 - \underline{\hspace{2cm}} =$

   $3 + \underline{\hspace{2cm}} =$

   $2 + \underline{\hspace{2cm}} =$

   3

7. $5 + \underline{\hspace{2cm}} =$

   $2 + \underline{\hspace{2cm}} =$

   $9 - \underline{\hspace{2cm}} =$

   6

8. $7 + \underline{\hspace{2cm}} =$

   $\underline{\hspace{2cm}} - 1 =$

   $\underline{\hspace{2cm}} - 3 =$

   8

9. $\underline{\hspace{2cm}} - 4 =$

   $8 - \underline{\hspace{2cm}} =$

   $3 + \underline{\hspace{2cm}} =$

   5

Write a contraction for each pair of words.

10. you are _____

11. do not _____

12. he is _____

13. I will _____

Write the two words that make up each contraction.

14. didn't _____

15. isn't _____

16. you've _____

17. she's _____

© Carson Dellosa Education

Language Arts & Grammar

Write *is* or *are* to complete each sentence.

1. We _____ going to town tomorrow.

2. This book _____ not mine.

3. Where _____ the box of cereal?

4. Owls _____ nocturnal.

5. _____ he planning to help?

6. _____ you going to the festival?

Add the correct ending punctuation to each sentence.

7. Are we going to the park _____

8. Look out for the ball _____

9. I know you can do it _____

10. Do bulls have horns on their heads _____

11. The girl on the bike is my sister _____

Write two sentences. Use two different ending punctuation marks.

_____

_____

_____

_____

DAY 16

Subtraction/Language Arts & Grammar

Subtract to find each difference.

12. 15   13. 14   14. 16   15. 17   16. 13
    − 4   − 2   − 8   − 3   − 4

17. 10   18. 18   19. 13   20. 11   21. 16
    − 4   − 7   − 6   − 9   − 5

Holidays and product names begin with a capital letter. Underline each letter that should be a capital three times like this: b.

22. On valentines day, Mom cooked a fancy dinner for Dad.

23. At the grocery store, we bought two boxes of tasty crunch granola bars.

24. We'll be back from vacation on labor day.

25. Scout and Otis are almost out of chicken nibblers dog treats.

 **Mindful Moment**

Make a list of things you can do to show respect to animals.

Geometry

DAY 17

Read each question. Circle the correct answer. Draw the shape in the box.

1. I have three sides and three angles. What am I?
    A. a quadrilateral
    B. a triangle
    C. a hexagon

2. I am a polygon. I have five equal sides and angles. What am I?
    A. a hexagon
    B. a cube
    C. a pentagon

3. I am a polygon. I have six equal sides and angles. What am I?
    A. a hexagon
    B. a cube
    C. a quadrilateral

4. I am a quadrilateral with four equal sides. My opposite sides and opposite angles are equal. What am I?
    A. a rhombus
    B. a triangle
    C. a pentagon

DAY 17

Addition/Language Arts & Grammar

Add to find each sum.

5. 8
    3
    5
    + 2
    ———

6. 2
    6
    4
    + 3
    ———

7. 1
    9
    2
    + 2
    ———

8. 6
    5
    1
    + 2
    ———

9. 2
    4
    3
    + 4
    ———

10. 3
    4
    5
    + 3
    ———

11. 5
    7
    2
    + 1
    ———

12. 6
    1
    8
    + 1
    ———

13. 0
    6
    1
    + 4
    ———

14. 4
    2
    3
    + 2
    ———

Pronouns take the place of nouns. A reflexive pronoun is a special type of pronoun that ends in *-self* or *-selves*. Circle the reflexive pronoun in each sentence.

15. Rico and I gave ourselves half an hour to get ready.

16. The children were proud of themselves for winning the game.

17. You know yourself better than anyone else does.

18. Josie tried to give herself a haircut when she was two!

19. I told myself not to be scared as I entered the dark room.

Money/Language Arts & Grammar

Draw a line to match the price of each toy with the correct amount of money.

1.

2.

3.

4.

Draw a line to match each contraction on the left to the word pair on the right that makes the contraction.

they will

she would

it is

he is

was not

Reading Comprehension

Mars

Have you ever dreamed of going to Mars? Mars is the fourth planet from the sun. A mineral gives the **surface** of Mars a red color. That's why it is called the "Red Planet."

A day on Mars is about the same length as it is on Earth. Mars has seasons, too. They last longer than Earth's seasons. This is because Mars is farther from the sun. It is much colder there. A summer day on Mars would feel like an icy cold winter day on Earth!

5. Why is Mars called the "Red Planet"?
   A. No one knows for sure.
   B. A mineral gives it a red color.
   C. The air on Mars is red.

6. What does *surface* mean?
   A. the top of
   B. the bottom of
   C. instead of

7. Why did the author write this passage?
   A. to tell a funny story about Mars
   B. so people would move to Mars
   C. to give some facts about Mars

Let's Play Today *See page 60.

Stand with your back to a wall. Slowly walk out your feet until you are in a sitting position. Now, stand back up.

Language Arts & Grammar/Reading Comprehension

Write the best adjective from the box to complete each sentence.

| funny | furry | hard | oak | red | six |

1. His kite got caught in that _____ tree.

2. I cannot believe you ate _____ apples.

3. We laughed at the _____ clowns.

4. Kayley got a _____ bike from her parents.

5. The ground by the tree is _____ and lumpy.

6. The rabbits all have soft and _____ ears.

Circle the main idea of each picture.

7.

   A. The children got very muddy.

   B. The boy is the youngest.

8.

   A. The girl is wearing a pink shirt.

   B. The children want to adopt a cat.

DAY 19

Money/Vocabulary

Circle the coins that add up to the amount shown.

9.

10¢

10.

16¢

11.

25¢

12.

45¢

Use the meanings of the prefixes to help you write the meaning of each word.

| un- = not | dis- = not, opposite of |
| re- = again | pre- = before |

13. unsafe = _____

14. rebuild = _____

15. dislike = _____

16. precook = _____

Addition & Subtraction/Measurement

DAY 20

Skill IDs: PD7 • F2U

Solve each problem.

1. 10
    − 4

2. 18
    − 14

3.   7
    − 3

4.   7
    + 5

5.   8
    + 2

6.   6
    − 4

7.   9
    − 4

8. 11
    − 1

9. 11
    + 8

10. 10
    − 8

Use an inch ruler to measure the pencils. Then, show the measurements on the line plot. For each pencil, draw an X above the number that shows its correct measurement.

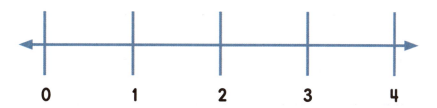

Fast Fun Fact

Dust from Africa can travel all the way to Florida.

DAY 20

Skill ID **J5D** — Search for this skill ID on IXL.com for more practice!

Reading Comprehension/Writing

Read each sentence. Follow the directions.

Draw a plate on a place mat.

Draw a napkin on the left side of the plate.

Draw a fork on the napkin.

Draw a knife and spoon on the right side of the plate.

Draw a glass of juice above the knife and spoon.

Draw your favorite lunch on the plate.

If I could fly anywhere, I would fly to _____

_____

_____

_____

_____

_____

_____

100 © Carson Dellosa Education

Science Experiment BONUS

Super Sediment*

What sinks to the bottom of a river first—soil, sand, or pebbles?

Materials:
- 3 paper cups
- sand
- funnel
- soil
- pebbles
- water
- soda bottle (2-liter with cap)

Procedure:
1. Fill one paper cup with soil, one cup with sand, and one cup with pebbles. These will be the sediment.
2. Use the funnel to pour the soil, sand, and pebbles into the bottle. Pour water into the bottle until it is almost full. Close the cap tightly.
3. Shake the bottle until everything is mixed well.
4. Place the bottle on a table. On a separate sheet of paper, draw a picture of what you see in the bottle. Watch as the sediment begins to settle in the bottle.
5. Check the bottle after 15–30 minutes. Draw what you see.
6. Check the bottle again in 24 hours. Draw what you see.

What's This All About?
Sediment is the soil, sand, and pebbles that wash into streams, rivers, and lakes. In nature, sediment piles up and forms sedimentary rocks.

In the bottle, you have created a small body of water with a lot of sediment. The larger pieces of sediment settle to the bottom more quickly. The smaller pieces of sediment are more likely to float in the water longer and settle to the bottom more slowly.

Think About It
- What is a funnel? Why do you need to use one to get the materials into the bottle?
- Which section of the experiment tells you what to do?

*See page 2.

Science Experiment

Sweet, Sour, Salty, Bitter*

Did you know that you can make a taste map of your tongue?

Materials:
- lemon (cut in half)
- pretzel
- water
- grapefruit rind
- sugar cube

Procedure:
1. Touch the inside of a lemon to the very tip of your tongue. Do you taste it? Don't move your tongue around. Rinse your mouth with water. Touch the lemon to the middle of your tongue. Do you taste it? Rinse your mouth with water. Touch the lemon to the sides of your tongue. Do you taste it?
2. Rinse your mouth with water. Repeat the activity with the pretzel, the grapefruit, and finally the sugar cube.

What's This All About?
There are four main tastes that humans can tell apart: sweet, sour, salty, and bitter. Your tongue is divided into different taste zones. Each taste zone is a certain area of your tongue. In this activity, you should discover which parts of your tongue detect each kind of taste.

More Fun Ideas to Try:
Based on your experiment, draw a taste map of your tongue. First, draw a picture of your tongue in the box. Then, label each area where you tasted salty, sweet, sour, and bitter.

*See page 2.

Social Studies Activity

Look What I Did!

A time line is a list of dates that tells important things that have happened. You have already had a lot of things happen in your lifetime. Make a time line to show your accomplishments, milestones, and important events. Ask an adult to help you. If you have a baby book, scrapbooks, photo albums, or other records, use those things to help, too. You will need a piece of poster board and markers to create the time line. List at least 10 different events to show a variety of activities. If possible, attach photos or drawings to highlight the events. This is a fun way to look back at your history. Display the time line in a special place in your bedroom. Add to it as you grow and do more.

Search for this skill ID on IXL.com for more practice!

Social Studies Activity

Sandbox Relief Map*

Some maps help people find their way. Other maps show physical features (things like oceans and mountains) of places. These are called relief maps. Make your own relief map in a sandbox. Get out your shovel and pail to dig and build. Be sure to make features such as a mountain, a lake, a river, a hill, an ocean, an island, a volcano, a desert, a forest, and a valley. Add water to fill up the water features. Use things that you find in nature, such as rocks, to build the mountains. Find some small sticks for trees and bushes. Soon, you will have your own real-life relief map.

*See page 2.

Social Studies Activity

Having a Ball on Earth

A globe is a 3D map that shows what Earth looks like. Make your own globe with a beach ball or large plastic ball and markers. Draw a line around the middle of the ball to represent the equator. The equator is a pretend line that marks the middle of the world. Label the top of the ball *north pole* and the bottom of the ball *south pole*. The north and south poles are places that mark the top and bottom of Earth. Draw and label the seven continents (Africa, Antarctica, Asia, Australia, Europe, North America, and South America) and the four major oceans (Arctic, Atlantic, Indian, and Pacific). Place a star sticker on the globe to represent the place where you live. Toss the globe around with a friend or family member, and try to learn the names of the important places that you marked. Soon, you will know more about Earth than you did before.

SECTION 3

Monthly Goals

Think of three goals to set for yourself this month. For example, you may want to do 30 math problems in one minute. Have an adult help you write your goals on the lines.

Place a sticker next to each of your goals that you complete. Feel proud that you have met your goals!

1. _____ PLACE STICKER HERE

2. _____ PLACE STICKER HERE

3. _____ PLACE STICKER HERE

Word List

The following words are used in this section. Read each word aloud with an adult. When you see a word from this list on a page, circle it with your favorite color of crayon.

cause   hundred

collect   map

effect   opinion

energy   subtract

fact   sum

Introduction to Endurance

This section includes Let's Play Today and Mindful Moments activities that focus on endurance. These activities are designed to help your child develop mental and physical stamina. If your child has limited mobility, feel free to modify any suggested activity or choose a different one from the list on the following page.

Let's Play Today

Many children seem to have endless energy and can run, jump, and play for hours. But endurance does not come naturally to everyone. Developing endurance requires regular exercise that gets the body moving and the heart pumping, like arm punches, jumping jacks, dancing, and playing sports.

Encourage your child to make exercise a part of their everyday routine during the summer. Give them suggestions of things that get them breathing harder and moving their body, such as playing hopscotch, going for a walk, kicking a ball with someone, climbing on playground equipment, riding a bike, and more.

Mindful Moments

Endurance applies to the mind as well as to the body. Explain to your child that endurance means to stick with something. For example, when someone feels like giving up at something but perseveres and finishes the task, they have demonstrated endurance.

To help your child practice mental endurance, identify an example of when they wanted to quit a task. Maybe your child didn't like the new game they were playing or the new skill they were practicing, and they wanted to quit. Talk about how it often takes people a while to learn something new, and if people always quit instead of persevering through a challenge, nobody would ever learn anything new or grow as a person. Emphasize that endurance and perseverance build character and make people mentally strong, and quitting should be a last resort. Developing endurance at a young age will serve your child well throughout life.

Engaging Online Practice

Bring learning to life with fun, interactive activities on IXL! Look for the Skill ID box and type the 3-digit code into the search bar on IXL.com or the IXL mobile app. Ten questions per day are free!

IXL Skill IDs: 5UN • D9K

© Carson Dellosa Education

SECTION 3

Let's Play Today

Get your child up and moving with these Let's Play Today activities. Section 3 focuses on endurance. Endurance is being able to complete many repetitions of a task, such as 10 jumping jacks, or perform an activity for an extended amount of time, such as riding a bike for 10 minutes. Building your child's endurance will help them get through everyday tasks and find success with physical activities and sports. Use this list in addition to or as a replacement for any Let's Play Today suggestions on the activity pages. This list was developed to be inclusive of a variety of abilities. Choose the ones that suit your child the best! These activities may require adult supervision. See page 2 for full caution information.

Jump Rope:
Start by jumping rope for 30 seconds. Jump rope every day and try to increase the amount of time you can jump every day.

Freeze Dance:
Have one person control the music. Ask them to play a favorite song. Dance while the music plays. When the music pauses, stop dancing. If you dance after the music stops, the person controlling the music assigns an endurance challenge (5 jumping jacks, push-ups, etc.). Then you can rejoin the game.

Scavenger Hunt Hike:
Go on a scavenger hunt hike. Create a list of things you think you might see, such as a traffic light, a dog, or a particular type of flower. Cross items off your list as you go. You can also build endurance by going on a simple walk or run.

Fun on Wheels:
Go on a bike ride or play bike games. This works great with wheelchairs too. Create an obstacle course of cones and weave in and out, challenge a friend to a bike race, or use chalk to create roads, stop signs, and more.

Let's Go Team:
Playing team sports is a great way to build endurance. Basketball, soccer, football, softball, baseball, volleyball, and more are all great ways to improve endurance. Choose a favorite team sport and get a group of kids together to play at a local park.

© Carson Dellosa Education

Addition/Spelling

Complete each table.

1. Add 10

5	15
8	
7	
9	
3	
4	

2. Add 8

2	
6	
4	
7	
3	
5	

3. Add 6

10	
6	
8	
7	
4	
5	

Circle the word that is spelled correctly in each row.

4. buy   buye   biy
5. liht   light   ligte
6. wonce   onse   once
7. carry   carey   carre
8. you're   yure   yo're

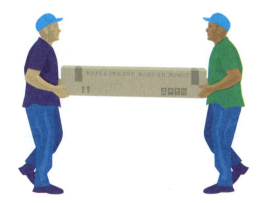

 **Mindful Moment**

Discuss with an adult two things you can do the next time you feel like quitting.

Reading Comprehension/Phonics

Read the story. Then, answer the questions.

   Once, there were two frogs who lived in a marsh. On a very hot summer day, the marsh dried up. The frogs had to look for another place to live. After some time, they found a deep well. "What a nice, cool, damp spot," said one frog. "Let us jump in and make ourselves at home."

   The other frog was wiser. "Not so fast, dear friend. What if this well dries up like the marsh? How would we ever get out again?"

9. What is the moral of this story?
    A. A penny saved is a penny earned.
    B. Look before you leap.
    C. Slow and steady wins the race.

10. What is the point of the fable?
    A. to teach a lesson
    B. to change the reader's mind about something
    C. to give directions

Write each word from the box under the word that has the same vowel sound.

| coat | drove | fox | job |
| rock | rope | those | top |

nose   **pop**

_____   _____

_____   _____

_____   _____

_____   _____

110

Subtraction/Language Arts & Grammar

IXL Skill IDs **8C3 • XM2**

DAY 2

Complete each table.

1.

Subtract 5	
9	4
5	
7	
10	
11	
8	

2.

Subtract 3	
10	
9	
7	
8	
6	
11	

3.

Subtract 2	
11	
7	
9	
5	
8	
6	

Combine each pair of sentences into a compound sentence. Use the conjunction in parentheses ( ). Make sure to put a comma before each conjunction.

4. Roman mowed the yard. He didn't weed the garden. (but)

Roman mowed the yard, but he didn't weed the garden.

5. Jackson made a fruit salad. Lena brought dessert. (and)

_____

6. The bunny hopped across the yard. The cat did not see it. (but)

_____

7. I could hear the rain on the roof. I knew the storm had begun. (so)

_____

8. Julia walks to school with Chase. She rides the bus. (or)

_____

© Carson Dellosa Education

DAY 2

Problem Solving/Spelling

Use the mileage maps to answer the questions.

9. How many miles is it from Salt Lake City to Bountiful? _____

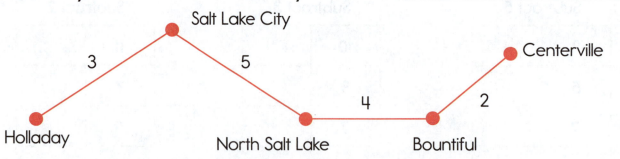

10. How many miles is it from Provo to Pleasant Grove? _____

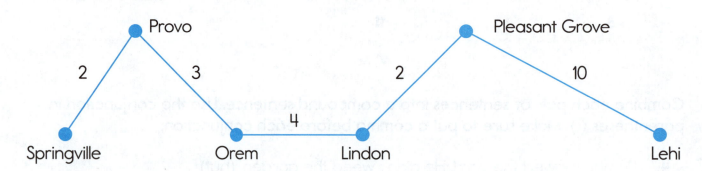

Read each sentence. If the underlined word is spelled correctly, circle *yes*. If the underlined word is not spelled correctly, circle *no*.

11.	The United States flag is red, white, and <u>bloo</u>.	yes	no
12.	Those girls were in my <u>class</u>.	yes	no
13.	Gina is a very <u>helpfull</u> friend.	yes	no
14.	I turned off the <u>light</u>.	yes	no
15.	This glue is sticky <u>stuf</u>.	yes	no
16.	Is <u>shee</u> coming with us?	yes	no

Addition/Measurement

Skill IDs: GLX • YRD

DAY 3

Solve each problem.

1. 29
   +12

2. 28
   +43

3. 67
   +26

4. 42
   +39

5. 89
   +11

6. 76
   +24

7. 66
   +24

8. 91
   + 9

9. 58
   +33

10. 46
   +16

Measure each item in centimeters. Then, answer the questions.

11.

How long is the fish? _____

How long is the saw? _____

How much longer is the fish than the saw? _____

12.

How long is the guitar? _____

How long is the violin? _____

How much longer is the guitar than the violin? _____

© Carson Dellosa Education

113

DAY 3

Place Value

Count the hundreds, tens, and ones. Write the number.

13.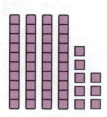

_____ hundreds, _____ tens, and _____ ones = _____

14.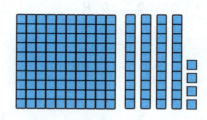

_____ hundred, _____ tens, and _____ ones = _____

15.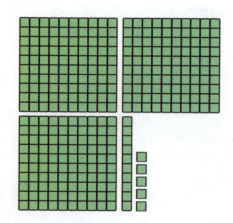

_____ hundreds, _____ ten, and _____ ones = _____

16.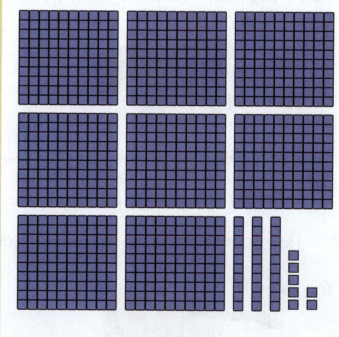

_____ hundreds, _____ tens, and _____ ones = _____

 Let's Play Today *See page 108.

Hop on one foot and then the other 10 times.

Numbers/Problem Solving

Write the numeral for each number word.

1. nine hundred nintey-six _____
2. twenty-one _____
3. eighty-two _____
4. thirty-seven _____
5. two hundred sixty-five _____
6. six hundred sixty-one _____
7. seventy-nine _____
8. fifty-eight _____
9. twenty-two _____
10. seven hundred eighty _____
11. one hundred eighteen _____
12. one hundred _____

Solve each problem.

13. Silas is 54 inches tall. Lily is 8 inches shorter than he is. How tall is Lily?

14. Anton picked 18 sunflowers, Luis picked 14, and Lola picked 26. How many sunflowers did they pick in all?

15. Noah and Aylen are collecting canned food for a food drive. On Monday, they collected 56 cans. On Tuesday, they collected 36 cans. How many cans did they collect in all?

16. Kris saved up $45. He decided to buy a skateboard for $27. How much money did he have left?

© Carson Dellosa Education

115

Reading Comprehension

Read the poem

My Cat

Have you seen my cat?
Yes, I've seen your cat.

Really? My cat is big.
I saw a big cat.

My cat has stripes.
I saw a big cat with stripes.

My cat's stripes are white.
I saw a big cat with white stripes.

My cat runs fast.
I saw a big cat with white stripes running fast.

You did see my cat! Where is it?
I don't know. I saw it last week.

Draw a line to connect each word to its antonym.

17. big   black

18. slow   little

19. white   fast

Answer the questions.

20. What is the poem about? _____

21. Describe the cat. _____

_____

Place Value/Phonics

Color the shape whose number matches each description.

1.

three hundreds, two tens, and three ones

2.

five hundreds, one ten, and seven ones

3.

five hundreds, nine tens, and zero ones

4.

two hundreds, six tens, and zero ones

5.

three hundreds, nine tens, and three ones

6.

one hundred, zero tens, and zero ones

Write each word from the box under the word that has the same vowel sound.

| blow | bowl | brown | clown | crown |
| elbow | how | mow | own | tower |

cow   pillow

_____   _____

_____   _____

_____   _____

_____   _____

_____   _____

DAY 5

Reading Comprehension/Writing

Write the letter of each cause beside its effect.

Effects   **Causes**

7. _____ Justin put on his mittens.   A. It was cold outside.

8. _____ Chloe put ice in the water.   B. Her feet had grown.

9. _____ Ahmet gave his dog a bath.   C. The bike's tires were flat.

10. _____ Evan put air in his bike tires. D. The rabbit was hungry.

11. _____ Kari got a new pair of shoes.   E. The water was warm.

12. _____ The rabbit ate the carrot.   F. The dog played in the mud.

Imagine that you are going on a trip. You can take only one thing. What would you take? Why?

_____

_____

_____

_____

_____

_____

Fast Fun Fact

Sloths move so slowly that green algae can grow on their fur.

Patterning  DAY 6

Circle the correct rule for each number pattern.

1. 2, 4, 6, 8, 10, 12

   +2   +1

2. 20, 18, 16, 14, 12, 10

   -2   -3

3. 50, 60, 70, 80, 90, 100

   -10   +10

4. 80, 79, 78, 77, 76, 75

   +10   -1

5. 35, 40, 45, 50, 55, 60

   +10   +5

6. 27, 24, 21, 18, 15, 12

   -2   -3

Mindful Moment

Next time you think, "I can't do it," pause and take a deep breath. Then, switch your thought to "I can't do it YET."

Reading Comprehension

Read the passage. Answer the questions.

Stamp Collecting

Are you a **philatelist**? If you collect stamps, that is what you are! Stamp collecting is a fun and interesting hobby.

If you want to start collecting stamps, you will need a few supplies. You will need a pair of tweezers to move the stamps so that they do not get dirty. You will also need an album with plastic pages to store your stamps.

Start by collecting some stamps. The stamps you collect can be new or used. You can collect stamps from letters that are delivered to your house. You can also buy stamps to add to your collection.

Next, decide how to sort your stamps. You can group them by their value, by the places they are from, or by the types of pictures on them. Then, place the stamps in your album.

Keep your stamp album in a cool, dry place away from direct sunlight. Heat, sun, and dampness can ruin your stamps.

7. Which sentence tells the main idea of the passage?
   A. Stamp collecting is a fun and interesting hobby.
   B. You can organize stamps in many different ways.
   C. Stamps come from all over the world.

8. What is a *philatelist*? _____

9. What is the main idea of the third paragraph?

10. Why did the author write this selection?

120 © Carson Dellosa Education

Geometry/Vocabulary

Write a number on each line to tell how many parts of the shape are colored.

1.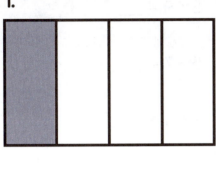

_____ fourth

2.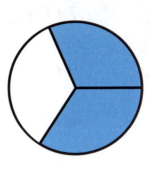

_____ thirds

3.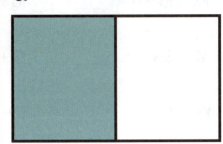

_____ half

Complete each sentence with the correct compound word from the word bank.

| cartwheel | fireworks | grandfather |
| snowflakes | sunflower | waterfall |

4. The _____ lit up the night sky.

5. My mother's dad is my _____ .

6. In gym class, we learned how to do a _____ .

7. The _____ is a large, yellow flower.

8. When the first _____ fall, we know winter is coming.

9. We pitched our tent near a beautiful _____ .

DAY 7

Skill IDs DF7 • ZDC

Addition/Reading Comprehension

Solve each problem. Circle the largest sum in each row.

10. 16 + 4 = ____   10 + 9 = ____   7 + 8 = ____   8 + 9 = ____

11. 8 + 8 = ____   13 + 6 = ____   9 + 9 = ____   5 + 7 = ____

12. 6 + 13 = ____   5 + 5 = ____   9 + 4 = ____   7 + 9 = ____

13. 8 + 3 = ____   12 + 2 = ____   4 + 15 = ____   6 + 7 = ____

Read the story. Circle each answer that makes sense. There may be more than one answer.

14. Murphy's mom quickly pulled everything out of the dryer. Then, she lifted the lid of the washer, looked inside, and shook her head. She looked around the kitchen and family room, and then she rushed upstairs. "I cannot find it," she called to Murphy. "The last time I saw it was after the game on Saturday. We have to find it before 4:00!"

   A. Murphy's mom has friends coming over at 4:00.
   B. Murphy's mom is looking for Murphy's soccer jersey.
   C. Murphy has a game today at 4:00.
   D. Murphy's mom lost her purse.

© Carson Dellosa Education

Measurement  DAY 8

Measure each object. Write the length in inches and in centimeters.

1.    _____ in.
   _____ cm

2.    _____ in.
   _____ cm

3.    _____ in.
   _____ cm

4.    _____ in.
   _____ cm

 **Let's Play Today** *See page 108.

Grab some streamers and tape. Ask an adult to help you tape together an obstacle course in a hallway or other narrow room. Crawl over and under without tearing a streamer.

© Carson Dellosa Education   123

DAY 8 — Problem Solving/Reading Comprehension

Use the chart to answer each question.

Allowance for Each Chore Completed

Bundle cardboard for recycling	$0.25
Empty wastepaper baskets	$0.75
Put away groceries	$0.50
Wash the car	$2.00
Set the table	$1.00

5. Which chore pays the most money? _____

6. If Hugo sets the table for dinner every night this week, how much will he earn? _____

7. Davis bundled cardboard for recycling two times this week. How much money did he earn? _____

Read each statement. Write *Y* for *yes* or *N* for *no* beside each statement.

How a Snake Is Like a Turtle

8. _____ Both have shells.

9. _____ Both can be on land.

10. _____ Both are reptiles.

11. _____ Both have scales.

How a Bike Is Like a Truck

12. _____ Both have tires.

13. _____ Both need gas.

14. _____ Both can be new.

15. _____ Both have four wheels.

Geometry/Graphing

DAY 9

Follow the directions to color the shapes.

1.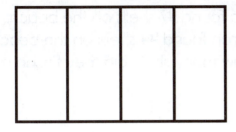

   Color three-fourths.

2.

   Color one-third.

3.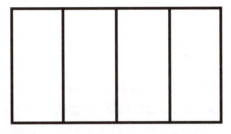

   Color one-fourth.

4.

   Color two-thirds.

The bar graph shows concession stand sales at a baseball game. Use the bar graph to answer the questions.

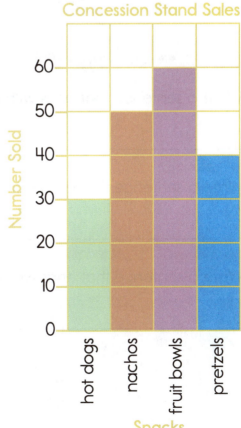

5. Do people buy more nachos or fruit bowls?

   _____

6. How many more fruit bowls than pretzels were sold? _____

7. People bought more than 50 of which item?

   _____

© Carson Dellosa Education

125

DAY 9

Problem Solving/Language Arts & Grammar

Solve each problem.

8. There are 26 students on one bus. There are 29 students on the other bus. How many students are on the buses altogether?

9. Nia found 47 shells on the beach. Byron found 44 shells on the beach. How many shells did they find in all?

10. Kamal ran 15 laps on Monday. He ran 17 laps on Tuesday. How many laps did Kamal run altogether?

11. Thomas saw 48 fish in one fish tank. Brooke saw 36 fish in another fish tank. How many fish did they see in all?

12. Write a sentence that ends with a period (.).

_____

13. Write a sentence that ends with a question mark (?).

_____

14. Write a sentence that ends with an exclamation point (!).

_____

Addition & Subtraction

DAY 10

Use each fact family to write two addition and two subtraction number sentences.

1. (6, 7, 13)

____ + ____ = ____

____ + ____ = ____

____ − ____ = ____

____ − ____ = ____

2. (7, 8, 15)

____ + ____ = ____

____ + ____ = ____

____ − ____ = ____

____ − ____ = ____

3. (10, 7, 17)

____ + ____ = ____

____ + ____ = ____

____ − ____ = ____

____ − ____ = ____

4. (6, 8, 14)

____ + ____ = ____

____ + ____ = ____

____ − ____ = ____

____ − ____ = ____

5. (7, 5, 12)

____ + ____ = ____

____ + ____ = ____

____ − ____ = ____

____ − ____ = ____

6. (5, 6, 11)

____ + ____ = ____

____ + ____ = ____

____ − ____ = ____

____ − ____ = ____

Fast Fun Fact

Jiffy is a real unit of time. It stands for one-hundredth of a second!

© Carson Dellosa Education

127

DAY 10

IXL Skill ID **ZXK**

Search for this skill ID on IXL.com for more practice!

Time

Use the calendars to answer each question.

May

S	M	T	W	TH	F	S
			1	2	3	4
5	6	7	8	9	10	11
12	13	14	15	16	17	18
19	20	21	22	23	24	25
26	27	28	29	30	31	

June

S	M	T	W	TH	F	S
						1
2	3	4	5	6	7	8
9	10	11	12	13	14	15
16	17	18	19	20	21	22
23	24	25	26	27	28	29
30						

7. Julia went to the dentist on the third Tuesday in May. What was the date?

Tuesday, May _____

8. Heath started his dance class on the first Monday in June. What was the date?

Monday, June _____

9. Today is May 10. Adam's family will see a play next Thursday. On what date will they see a play?

Thursday, May _____

10. How many days are between May 29 and June 5?

_____

128

© Carson Dellosa Education

| Addition | | IXL Skill ID **W8T** | DAY **11** |

Write a repeated addition equation to find the total number of items in each group.

1.

_____

2.

_____

3.

_____

4.
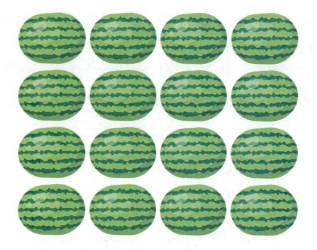
_____

Mindful Moment

What is one thing you can do now that you could not do in kindergarten? Tell a family member.

© Carson Dellosa Education

129

Language Arts & Grammar/Vocabulary

Some nouns name groups of people, animals, or things. Choose a noun from the word bank to complete each sentence.

| class | family | school | herd |

5. My _____ lives at 123 Maple Street.

6. We saw a _____ of cattle grazing in the field.

7. A _____ of fish swam under the dock.

8. On Wednesday, our _____ will take a field trip.

An *analogy* is a way to show how things are alike. Look at the first set of words. Decide how they are related. Apply that relationship to the second set of words.

Finger : *hand* :: *toe* : _____ . (Think: A *finger* is part of a *hand*. What is a *toe* part of? The answer is *foot*.)

Use the words from the word bank to complete each analogy.

| light | sky | square | table |

9. sleep : bed :: eat : _____

10. three : triangle :: four : _____

11. green : grass :: blue : _____

12. win : loss :: dark : _____

130 © Carson Dellosa Education

Problem Solving/Phonics

Solve each problem.

1. Claire ate a snack at 10:00. She ate lunch 2 hours later. What time did she eat lunch?

   _____

2. This morning, Hau read for 15 minutes. He started at 9:00. What time did he finish reading?

   _____

3. Recess lasted 30 minutes. It started at 2:00. What time did it end?

   _____

4. Ellis left school at 3:30. He rode the bus for 30 minutes. What time did he get off the bus?

   _____

Say each word aloud. Write the syllables in the boxes.

5. apartment

6. enormous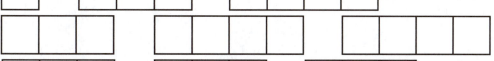

7. subtraction

8. wonderful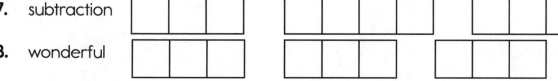

Addition/Reading Comprehension

Solve each problem. Use the number line to help you add hundreds.

9. 300 + 200 = _____   10. 700 + 200 = _____

11. 100 + 200 = _____   12. 600 + 400 = _____

13. 400 + 400 = _____   14. 500 + 200 = _____

Read the table of contents. Write the chapter and page number where you should begin looking for the answer to each question.

Table of Contents

Chapter 1	Mammals (Animals with Fur)	3
Chapter 2	Reptiles (Snakes, Turtles, and Alligators)	13
Chapter 3	Amphibians (Frogs and Toads)	21
Chapter 4	Fish	35
Chapter 5	Insects and Spiders	49
Chapter 6	Birds	57

15. How long do lions live? Chapter _____ Page _____

16. How fast do sailfish swim? Chapter _____ Page _____

17. What color is a robin's egg? Chapter _____ Page _____

18. Do spiders bite? Chapter _____ Page _____

© Carson Dellosa Education

Reading Comprehension

DAY 13

Read the story. Fill in the table.

Today is Rachel's birthday. She invited four friends to her party. Each friend brought a gift. Rachel's brother mixed up the tags on the gifts. Can you use the clues to put the tags on the correct gifts?

Grace's gift has flowered wrapping paper and a bow.
Kate's gift is small and has a bow.
Meghan forgot to put a bow on her gift.
Jade's gift has striped wrapping paper.

Write O in the box when you know a gift was brought by the girl.
Write X in the box when you know a gift was not brought by the girl.

Kate				
Grace				
Jade				
Meghan				

Let's Play Today *See page 108.

Play a game of leapfrog with a friend or family member. See how many times you can leap.

Search for this skill ID on IXL.com for more practice!

Reading Comprehension

Read the story.

Aunt Antonym

We have a nickname for my mother's sister. We call her Aunt Antonym. She always says or does the opposite of what we say or do. One day, we all went to the zoo. At the monkey exhibit, we thought the monkeys were cute. My aunt thought that they were strange. Soon, we were hungry. My aunt was still full from breakfast. After lunch, we rode the train around the zoo. My aunt wanted to walk. Finally, my aunt said that she was tired and ready to go. We were still full of energy. We wished we could have stayed.

Write *T* next to each statement that is true. Write *F* next to each statement that is false.

1. _____ The author is writing about their sister.

2. _____ Aunt Antonym is the real name of the author's aunt.

3. _____ Aunt Antonym was full from breakfast.

4. _____ Aunt Antonym did not want to ride the train.

Write a word from the story that is an antonym for each word.

5. ride _____ 6. stay _____

7. energetic _____ 8. hungry _____

9. From whose point of view is the story told?
    A. Aunt Antonym
    B. Aunt Antonym's niece or nephew
    C. a monkey at the zoo

Subtraction/Writing

Follow the directions to solve each problem.

1. Start with 800. Write the number that is 200 less. _____
2. Start with 600. Write the number that is 300 less. _____
3. Start with 200. Write the number that is 100 less. _____
4. Start with 700. Write the number that is 500 less. _____
5. Start with 900. Write the number that is 400 less. _____
6. Start with 600. Write the number that is 100 less. _____

Imagine that you are an adult for a day. Make a list of things that you would do that you cannot do now as a child.

_____
_____
_____
_____
_____
_____
_____
_____
_____

DAY 14

Patterning/Writing

Complete each number pattern. Write the rule.

7. 2, 4, 6, 8, _____, _____, _____, _____, _____, _____

    Rule: _____

8. 10, 20, 30, _____, _____, _____, _____, _____, _____

    Rule: _____

9. 5, 10, 15, _____, _____, _____, _____, _____, _____

    Rule: _____

10. 3, 6, 9, 12, _____, _____, _____, _____, _____, _____

    Rule: _____

Pretend that you are planning a Silly Saturday party. Write a letter to invite someone to your party.

Dear _____,

_____

_____

_____

Your friend,

_____

Addition/Vocabulary

Add to find each sum.

1.   3
     3
   + 3

2.   2
     2
   + 2

3.   4
     4
   + 4

4.   5
     5
   + 5

5.   3
     3
     3
   + 3

6.   2
     2
     2
   + 2

7.   5
     5
     5
   + 5

8.   4
     4
     4
   + 4

A glossary is found at the back of a book. It tells what certain words in the book mean. Use this glossary from a book about deserts to answer the questions below.

arid something that is very dry
camouflage coloring that helps an animal hide
desert an environment where very little rain falls; home to few plants and animals
evaporate to change from a liquid into a gas
precipitation any kind of water that falls from the sky (like rain, snow, hail, etc.)

9. What does *evaporate* mean? _____

_____

10. A moth that blends in with the bark on a tree is using _____.

11. If a place is arid, it is very _____.

12. What is one example of precipitation? _____

© Carson Dellosa Education

137

Write the expanded form for each number.

13. 251 = _____ hundreds + _____ tens + _____ one = _____ + _____ + _____

14. 341 = _____ hundreds + _____ tens + _____ one = _____ + _____ + _____

15. 563 = _____ hundreds + _____ tens + _____ ones = _____ + _____ + _____

16. 752 = _____ hundreds + _____ tens + _____ ones = _____ + _____ + _____

Use the number line to help you solve each problem. Mark the number line to show your work.

17. 25 + 40 = _____

18. 56 + 18 = _____

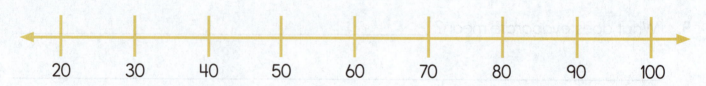

Fast Fun Fact

Butterflies and moths are found on every continent except Antarctica.

Reading Comprehension

Read the passage. Answer the questions.

How Plants Grow

A plant needs **energy** to grow. Energy comes from food. A plant makes its food in its leaves. Sunlight and water help the plant make food. After you plant a seed, a tiny seedling pushes its way out from the soil. The plant grows toward the sun. The plant must get water, or it will dry out and die. The roots of the plant pull water and nutrients from the soil. If there is little rain where you live, you may need to water your plant. If the soil in your area has few nutrients, you may need to add plant food to the soil. That way, your plant gets what it needs.

1. What is the main idea of this passage?
    - A. A plant can die without water.
    - B. Plants need food, water, and sunlight to grow.
    - C. Plants start as seeds.

2. What happens after you plant a seed? _____
   _____

3. Where does energy come from? _____
   _____

4. When might you need to water your plant? _____
   _____

5. Why is the word *energy* in bold print in the passage? _____
   _____

DAY 16

Language Arts & Grammar

Write *a* or *an* in front of each noun.

6. _____ mayor
7. _____ officer
8. _____ doctor
9. _____ scientist
10. _____ athlete
11. _____ explorer
12. _____ artist

Circle the adjective that describes each underlined noun.

13. Insects have six <u>legs</u>.
14. Bumblebees have hairy <u>bodies</u>.
15. A beetle has a hard <u>body</u>.
16. Ladybugs have black <u>spots</u>.
17. Butterflies can be beautiful <u>colors</u>.
18. Termites have powerful <u>jaws</u>.
19. Dragonflies have four <u>wings</u>.
20. A green <u>grasshopper</u> jumps away.

Mindful Moment

Imagine that you and a friend are placed in different classes for second grade. Talk to a family member about how it makes you feel.

140

© Carson Dellosa Education

Number Relationships

Write > or < to compare each pair of numbers.

1. 103 ◯ 111
2. 640 ◯ 460
3. 322 ◯ 100
4. 190 ◯ 910
5. 290 ◯ 300
6. 985 ◯ 852
7. 140 ◯ 400
8. 124 ◯ 216
9. 648 ◯ 846
10. 680 ◯ 480
11. 592 ◯ 324
12. 745 ◯ 746

Explain how you would compare two three-digit numbers.

_____
_____
_____
_____

Spelling/Reading Comprehension

Look up the words in a dictionary. In each pair, circle the word that is misspelled. Write the word correctly on the line.

13. early — thougt — _____
14. sents — picnic — _____
15. because — dragin — _____
16. chane — while — _____
17. speshal — coat — _____

Read the story.

Winter Fun

Some people like spring, but I do not. I think that winter is the best season. My family goes to the mountains every year. My stepmom is a good skier. She skis while we watch. My dad wears snowshoes and goes on long walks. My brothers and I like to play in the snow. The nights are too cold to be outside. So, we stay warm in our cabin. My stepmom makes us hot chocolate at bedtime, and we tell stories.

Decide whether each sentence is a fact or an opinion. Write F for *fact* or O for *opinion*.

18. _____ Winter is the best season.
19. _____ My family goes to the mountains.
20. _____ My stepmom makes us hot chocolate.
21. _____ I think my stepmom is a good skier.
22. _____ The nights are too cold.
23. _____ Dad goes on long walks.

Reading Comprehension

Search for this skill ID on IXL.com for more practice! **IXL** Skill ID **LTS**

DAY 18

Read the passage. Answer the questions.

The Moon

The moon lights up the night sky. Sometimes, the moon looks narrow. Sometimes, it looks round. The way the moon looks has to do with the position of the moon as viewed from Earth. When the moon is between the sun and Earth, the moon looks black. This is called a new moon. When Earth is between the sun and the moon, the moon looks bright and round. This is called a full moon. In the middle of these periods, half of the moon is lit, and half of the moon is dark. It takes about one month for the moon to finish the entire cycle.

1. What is the main idea of this passage?
   A. The moon can look thin or fat.
   B. The moon travels around Earth.
   C. The moon looks different during the month.

2. What makes the way the moon looks change? _____
   _____

3. When does a new moon happen? _____
   _____

4. What is the author's purpose for writing this passage?
   A. to tell facts about the way the moon looks
   B. to entertain the reader
   C. to encourage the reader to visit the moon

Let's Play Today *See page 108.

Imagine that you can only walk backward! For one minute, walk backward to move around your home.

© Carson Dellosa Education

143

Measurement/Reading Comprehension

Estimate the length of each item in centimeters. Then, measure to check your guess!

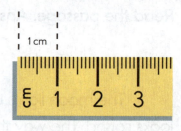

5. _____ cm

6. _____ cm

7. _____ cm

8. _____ cm

Read the story. Then, answer the questions.

Learning to Cook

My big brother is helping me learn to cook. I think he is an excellent cook. Last night, we made noodles with tomato sauce. We also made spinach bread. We planned to bake a pie, but we ran out of flour. Mom loved the meal. She said, "You boys are hired!"

9. Who is telling the story?
   A. the mother
   B. the older brother
   C. a boy who cooks with his big brother

10. Why didn't the boys bake a pie? _____

Reading Comprehension

Read the passage. Answer the questions.

Teeth

Teeth are important for chewing food, so you need to take care of your teeth. When you are a child, you have baby teeth. These fall out and are replaced by adult teeth. You can expect to have 32 teeth one day. You should brush your teeth at least twice a day—once in the morning and once at bedtime. Also, you should floss to remove food that gets stuck between your teeth. That way, you will have a healthy smile!

1. What is the main idea of this passage?
    - **A.** You can have a healthy smile.
    - **B.** It is important to take care of your teeth.
    - **C.** Adults have more teeth than children.

2. How does the author convince you to take good care of your teeth?
   _____

3. What happens to baby teeth? _____
   _____

4. How many teeth do adults have? _____

5. How often should you brush your teeth?
    - **A.** only at lunchtime
    - **B.** at least once a week
    - **C.** at least twice a day

DAY 19

IXL Skill IDs **2Q6 • T6U** Search for these skill IDs on IXL.com for more practice!

Subtraction/Vocabulary

Solve each problem.

6.	63 − 40	7.	80 − 60	8.	75 − 50	9.	79 − 20	10.	38 − 10

11.	93 − 30	12.	67 − 40	13.	83 − 20	14.	77 − 10	15.	76 − 50

Look up the words in a dictionary. Write the meanings on the lines.

16. absorb: _____

17. drowsy: _____

18. victory: _____

19. lasso: _____

20. jostle: _____

21. overcast: _____

22. merchant: _____

146 © Carson Dellosa Education

Graphing

Tara and her dad planted a tiny pine tree in their yard on her sixth birthday. They measured it every year on her birthday to see how many inches it had grown. Look at the graph and answer the questions.

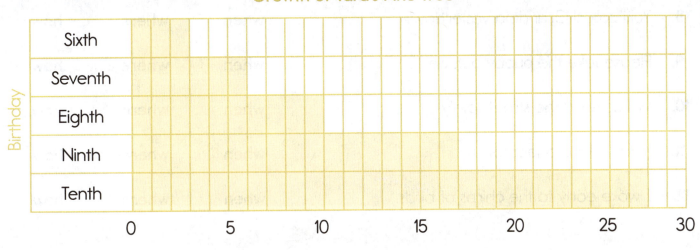

1. How tall was the tree when Tara planted it? _____

2. How tall was the tree on Tara's eighth birthday? _____

3. On which birthday was the tree 17 inches tall? _____

4. How many inches did the tree grow from Tara's seventh birthday to her eighth birthday? _____

5. How many inches did the tree grow from Tara's ninth birthday to her tenth birthday? _____

6. How many inches did the tree grow from Tara's seventh birthday to her ninth birthday? _____

 **Fast Fun Fact**

If a cranberry is ripe, it will bounce. Cranberries are also called *bounceberries*!

DAY 20

Language Arts & Grammar/Addition & Subtraction

Adverbs often answer the questions *where*, *when*, or *how*. Underline the adverb in each sentence. Then, circle *when*, *where*, or *how* to show what question it answers.

7. Mom and Dad clapped proudly for Shaun.   when   where   how

8. Yuki called Grandma yesterday.   when   where   how

9. Please take the puppy outside.   when   where   how

10. Will crossed the street safely.   when   where   how

11. Addy raced ahead of us.   when   where   how

12. I woke early to the chirps of birds.   when   where   how

Use the hundreds, tens, and ones blocks to help you solve each problem.

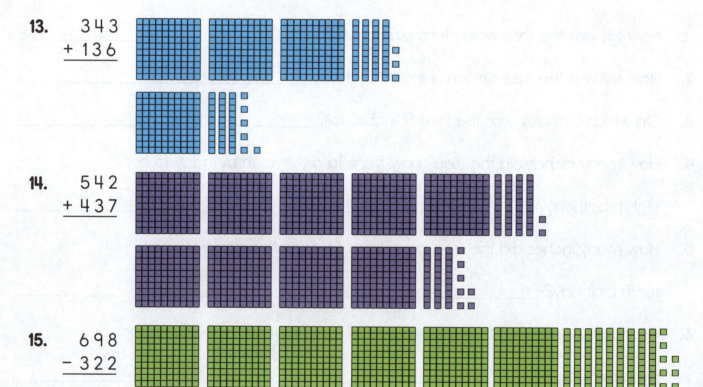

13. 343 + 136

14. 542 + 437

15. 698 − 322

Science Experiment

Catching Ice Cubes

Can you use salt and a piece of string to "catch" an ice cube?

Materials:
- ice cube
- salt
- string

Procedure:
1. Try to catch the ice cube with the piece of string. (You cannot tie the string around the ice cube.) Can you do it?

2. Next, place the string on the ice cube and sprinkle a little salt on the string. Count to 30 and slowly lift the string. The ice cube will be attached!

What's This All About?
When you sprinkle salt on the ice, it lowers the freezing temperature of the ice. This causes some water to melt around the string. When the water forms, it **dilutes** the salt on the ice and allows the water to freeze around the string. This is why you can pick it up.

Think About It
- Why do you have to count to 30 before you lift the string?
- In the last paragraph, what do you think *dilutes* mean?

BONUS — Science Experiment

Pinching Water

Can you hold two streams of water together? Or, can you separate two streams of water that had been flowing together? You would probably have to be pretty powerful! Or, would you?

Materials:
- nail (8- or 16-penny)
- hammer
- soup can (empty)
- masking tape

Procedure
1. Ask an adult to use a hammer and nail to make two small holes in the lower section of the soup can. The holes should be close to the bottom and 0.5 inches (1.27 cm) apart. Tape over the holes.
2. Fill the can with water and hold it over a sink. Then, remove the tape.
3. Using your fingers, try to pinch the two streams of water together.
4. Using your fingers, try to split the two streams of water.

What's This All About?
When you pinch the streams of water together, the water molecules act like magnets. They attract each other and form larger water drops.

By splitting the water streams, you push the streams far enough away that they cannot attract each other. When this happens, they stay separate. As long as you have water in the can, you will be able to pinch or split the streams of water.

Social Studies Activity

Animals Around the World

Studying animals is a great way to learn about different places in the world. Go to the library and check out books about animals that live in other parts of the world. Or, search the Internet with an adult to find out about animals. Choose an animal that lives on each continent (Africa, Antarctica, Asia, Australia, Europe, North America, and South America). As you read about each animal, you may find that the climate (weather patterns) or the food that grows in a place affects which animals live there. On the chart, write the name of each animal, the continent on which it lives, and why it lives there.

Animal	Continent	Why It Lives There

151

Social Studies Activity

Dessert Map*

A relief map shows the physical features of a place, such as rivers and mountains. Sometimes it is called a *topographical map*. You will call this a delicious map when you are finished with this activity!

Make this map in the kitchen with an adult's help. You will need two packages of prepared sugar cookie dough. You will also need some toppings, such as chocolate syrup, sliced fruit, and sprinkles.

Press the cookie dough from one package onto a cookie sheet. Use the other package of cookie dough to mold and shape land features. You could make mountains, hills, islands, volcanoes, deserts, forests, and valleys.

Bake the "map," following the directions on the package. Let the map cool. Use chocolate syrup to make water features, such as lakes and rivers. Highlight other features with different toppings.

Share the dessert with your family. Tell them what you learned about relief maps.

*See page 2.

Social Studies Activity

Earth Effects

Earth is a big place. Did you know that what you do every day can affect the planet? Almost every human action does something to Earth. Think about this: If a family goes to the beach for the day and leaves behind a few soft drink cans, a magazine, and an empty sunscreen bottle, they have had a negative effect on our planet. But, if they had simply taken the items with them and dropped them off in recycling bins, they would have had a positive effect on Earth. The metal cans, magazine, and sunscreen bottle could be recycled and made into something new. Trash would not have littered the beach. The ocean animals would not have been hurt by the trash left behind.

Do you want to have a positive effect on Earth? Have your family members help you make a list of things you can do to be good to the planet.

_____

_____

_____

_____

_____

_____

_____

© Carson Dellosa Education

BONUS

Reflect and Reset

Think back on your year of first grade. What was the hardest part? Write about it or draw a picture.

What was your favorite part? Write about it or draw a picture.

What are you most proud of? Write about it or draw a picture.

Reflect and Reset

Think ahead to your year of second grade. What might be a challenge? Write about it or draw a picture.

What are you looking forward to? Write about it or draw a picture.

Think of three goals that you would like to set for yourself for second grade. For example, you may want to join a new club, play a new sport, or improve in math. Write your goals on the lines.

1. _____

2. _____

3. _____

Answer Key

Section 1

Day 1/Page 13
1. sight—storm clouds moving in; 2. touch—tiny sprinkles on my face; 3. taste—little drops inside my mouth; 4. hearing—tapping a rhythm on the window; 5. smell—clean, fresh air; The capital letters should be written from A to Z.; 6. o; 7. a; 8. e; 9. u; 10. i; 11. o

Day 2/Page 15
1. 4; 2. 12; 3. 5; 4. 18; 5. 16; 6. 20; 7. 17; 8. 8; 9. 14; 10. 18; 11. Sanja ate soup for lunch.; 12. Eli will race down the hill.; 13. Abby splashes her brother in the pool.; 14. The piano needs to be tuned.; 15. Ty slammed the car door.; The lowercase letters should be written from a to z.; Drawings will vary.

Day 3/Page 17
1.

2.

3.

4. e; 5. o; 6. a; 7. i;

Base Word	Add -ed	Add -ing
8. jump	jumped	jumping
9. pat	patted	patting
10. open	opened	opening
11. start	started	starting
12. touch	touched	touching
13. blink	blinked	blinking

14. van; 15. mop; 16. slide

Day 4/Page 19
1. Students should color one-half of the rectangle.; 2. Students should color one-fourth of the circle.; 3. Students should color two-fourths of the rectangle.; 4. can; 5. pan; 6. pin; 7. cube; 8. kite; 9. cap; 10. 20; 11. 50; 12. 10; 13. 20; 14. 30; 15. 40; 16. ?; 17. ?; 18. .; 19. .; 20. ?; 21. ?; 22. !; 23. !; 24. .; 25. ?

Day 5/Page 21
1. 5 + 8 = 13, 13 − 8 = 5, 13 − 5 = 8; 2. 5 + 7 = 12, 7 + 5 = 12, 12 − 7 = 5, 12 − 5 = 7; 3. 8 + 6 = 14, 6 + 8 = 14, 14 − 8 = 6, 14 − 6 = 8; 4. o; 5. u; 6. a; 7. e; 8. a; 9. i; 10. 4; 11. 9; 12. 9; 13. 9; 14. 6; 15. 9; 16. 4; 17. 8; 18. Students should add a comma after August 5.; 19. Students should add a comma after April 18.; 20. Students should add a comma after August 11.; 21. Students should add a comma after June 4.; 22. Students should add a comma after October 23.

Day 6/Page 23
1. 24; 2. 40; 3. 33; 4. 57; 5. 26; 6. 45; 7. e; 8. a; 9. i; 10. e; 11. u; 12. o; 13. read; 14. angry; 15. kick; 16. watch; 17. smooth; 18. happy; Check student's list of words.

Day 7/Page 25
1. 15 train cars; 2. 8 deer; 3. 18 words; 4. 19 markers; 5. 4, 6; 6. 1, 9; 7. 8, 4; 8. 6, 4; 9. 40; 10. 11; 11. 93; 12. 28; 13. 17 flowers; 14. 18 animals; 15. 20 pieces of fruit; 16. 14 animals; 17. bow; 18. egg; 19. sun

Day 8/Page 27
1.–12. Students should circle the number sentences for numbers 1, 2, 5, 7, 8, 10, 11, and 12.; Answers will vary.; 13. dark; 14. girls; 15. hop; 16. wet; Answers will vary.

Day 9/Page 29
1. Possible answers: thick, heavy, quiet, thick, gray, blanket; 2. Xander's room and backyard; 3. Possible answer: Xander woke up. He went outside. It was a very foggy morning.; 4. D; 5. B; Answers will vary.

Day 10/Page 31
1. 20; 2. 70; 3. 40; 4. 10; 5. mail carrier; 6. doctor; 7. farmer; 8. pilot; 9. teacher; 10. baker; The following words should be colored blue: fry, tie, light, my, sigh, try, bike, sign, pie, guy, by, high, dry, bite, time, night, cry, dime, fine, lie, sight, why, right, shy, ride, buy, side, hike, kite, nine.; The following words should be colored green: bib, wig, six, if, fib, gift, pit, miss, fish, lit, chin, sit, hill, hid, bill, quit, bin, mitt, tin, win, fit, will, pin, fin, zip, did.; 11. backed, baked; 12. whent, went;

Answer Key

13. <u>trane</u>, train; **14.** <u>rom</u>, room

Day 11/Page 33
1. 5, 2, 3, 5; **2.** 9, 2, 7, 2; **3.** 8, 3, 5, 5, 3, 8, 5; **4.** 7 + 5; **5.** 6 + 9;
6. 5 + 8; **7.** C; **8.** 2, 1, 3

Day 12/Page 35
1. 4; **2.** 9; **3.** 10; **4.** 1; **5.** 1; **6.** 2; **7.** dr; **8.** tr; **9.** gr; **10.** cl; **11.** gl;
12. st; **13.** 19, 39; **14.** 80, 100; **15.** 3, 23; **16.** 65, 85; **17.** Ducks like
to swim.; **18.** Can we play in the sandbox?; **19.** Some birds
make nests in trees.; **20.** Are you having fun today?

Day 13/Page 37:
1. Students should underline the s in stella 3 times.;
2. Students should underline the r in rodrigo 3 times.;
3. Students should underline the k in kerry and a in august
3 times.; **4.** Students should underline the j in july 3 times.;
Students should circle the cake, whale, rake, and grapes.;
5. Peter's muffin; **6.** Kate's kite; **7.** Hasaan's hat; **8.** Sammy's
soccer ball; **9.** pink; **10.** red; **11.** pink; **12.** red

Day 14/Page 39
1. 9, 9, 4, 5; **2.** 2, 6, 8, 6, 2, 6; **3.** Answers will vary but may
include: 7, 3, 10, 3, 7, 10, 10, 7, 3, 10, 3, 7;

Common Nouns	Proper Nouns
hippo	Olivia
holiday	Greenlawn Library
cousin	Dr. Yang
store	Thanksgiving

4. C; **5.** B; **6.** his; **7.** their; **8.** her

Day 15/Page 41
1. 12 baseballs; **2.** 7 apples; **3.** 18 cookies; **4.** 6 kittens;
5. 13 cards; **6.** 14 seashells; **7.** C; **8.** 3, 1, 2

Day 16/Page 43
1. Q; **2.** E; **3.** C; **4.** S; **5.** S; **6.** and; **7.** or; **8.** so; **9.** but;
10. The bees are around the hive..; **11.** The bird loves to sing.;
12. 2; **13.** 1; **14.** 1; **15.** 2

Day 17/Page 45
1. melted; **2.** sweeter; **3.** untie; **4.** fearful; **5.** reread;
6. preheat; **7.** a; **8.** o; **9.** u; **10.** a; **11.** i; **12.** i; **13.** on top of;
14. next to; **15.** under; long a: great, break, steak; long e:
peach, leaf, beat

Day 18/Page 47
1. 2, 6; **2.** 4, 1; **3.** 4, 5; **4.** 8, 4; **5.** 6, 5; **6.** 7, 2; **7.** 1, 7; **8.** 3, 9;
9. 5, 0; **10.** 5, 1; **11.** 9, 7; **12.** 10, 0; Answers will vary.; **13.** 4;
14. 2; **15.** 5; **16.** 3; **17.** 1; Answers and drawings will vary.

Day 19/Page 49
1. <; **2.** >; **3.** <; **4.** >; **5.** >; **6.** >; **7.** >; **8.** <; **9.** <; **10.** <; **11.** >;
12. >; **13.** <; **14.** <; **15.** >; **16.** Students should draw a circle.;
17. Students should draw a triangle.; **18.** Students should
draw a square or a rhombus.; **19.** Students should draw
a square or a parallelogram.; **20.** ant; **21.** baby; **22.** key;
23. dog; Answers will vary.

Day 20/Page 51
1. 4:00; **2.** 11:00; **3.** 8:30; **4.** ch; **5.** wh; **6.** sh; 1, 3, 2; **7.** C;
8. A; **9.** B

Section 2

Day 1/Page 61
1. 65, 80, 85; **2.** 330, 360, 380; **3.** 500, 600, 800;
4.– **5.** Answers will vary.; **6.** The sun will shine today.;
7. I walked a mile today.; **8.** We painted our fence.;
9. She will knit something for me.; **10.** 154; **11.** 90; **12.** 122;
13. 75

Day 2/Page 63
1. 71; **2.** 91; **3.** 72; **4.** 34; **5.** 41; **6.** 40; **7.** 99; **8.** 80; **9.** 54;
10. glass; **11.** frog; **12.** clock; **13.** bowl; **14.** C; **15.** B;
16. did not; **17.** it is; **18.** we are; **19.** you have; **20.** do not;
21. we will; **22.** is not

Day 3/Page 65
1. 48¢; **2.** 62¢; **3.** 39¢; **4.** 25¢; Answers will vary.; **5.** 12;
6. 12; **7.** 10; **8.** 14; **9.** 20; **10.** 6; **11.** 5; **12.** 4; **13.** 0; **14.** 8;
15. state; **16.** rake; **17.** tag; **18.** call; **19.** gate

Day 4/Page 67
1. sipped; **2.** pounded; **3.** nervous; **4.** exhausted;
5. 12, even; **6.** 18, even; **7.** 9, odd; **8.** 5, odd

Long a	Long e	Long i
apron	eagle	rider
Monday	season	bedtime
flavor	fever	unkind

Long o	Long u
frozen	bugle
ocean	argue
hello	human

9. <u>yu</u>, you; **10.** <u>giv</u>, give; **11.** <u>sti</u>, sit; **12.** <u>miks</u>, mix

© Carson Dellosa Education

Answer Key

Day 5/Page 69
Answers will vary.; Check students' graphs..; **1.** Olivia lives on a farm.; **2.** Olivia wakes up early to do chores.; **3.** Answers will vary but may include: Olivia feeds the horses and the chickens, collects the eggs, and helps milk the cows.; **4.** Olivia's favorite thing to do in the morning is eat breakfast.; **5.** coin; **6.** boil; **7.** toy

Day 6/Page 71
1. 9; **2.** 3; **3.** 12; **4.** 15; **5.** 7; **6.** 7; **7.** 14; **8.** 9; **9.** 15; **10.** 12; **11.** 14; **12.** 30; **13.** 15 beads; **14.** 18 utensils

15.

16.

17.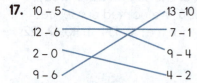

18.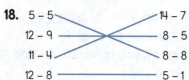

19. gift, his; **20.** car, flat; **21.** sat, the; **22.** dad, store

Day 7/Page 73
1. Sidney's umbrella is old.; **2.** Tabby is a farm cat.; **3.** I think it will snow.; **4.** 53 inches; **5.** 66°; **6.** 89 inches; **7.** 31 pounds; **8.** yes; **9.** no; **10.** yes; **11.** e; **12.** i; **13.** e; **14.** e; **15.** i; **16.** e; **17.** i; **18.** e; **19.** i; **20.** i; **21.** e; **22.** e

Day 8/Page 75
1. book; **2.** leg; **3.** cat; **4.** chair; **5.** apple; **6.** Tom; **7.** oy, boy; **8.** oi, oil; **9.** oi, soil; **10.** oi, voice; **11.** A; **12.** B; **13.** He keeps practicing.

Day 9/Page 77
1. sang; **2.** ring; **3.** is; **4.** ran; **5.** take; **6.** has; Answers will vary.; **7.** 28¢; **8.** 25 stamps; **9.** 28 fish; **10.** 23 balloons; children; mice; foot; men; tooth; person

Day 10/Page 79
1. 53; **2.** 97; **3.** 50; **4.** 57; **5.** 78; **6.** 79; **7.** sh; **8.** th; **9.** ch; **10.** 8, 10, 12; **11.** 8, 16, 20, 24; **12.** 10, 20, 25; **13.** it's; **14.** they've; **15.** we're; **16.** I'm; **17.** you'll; **18.** she'll

Day 11/Page 81
1. Students should divide rectangle into 3 rows and 4 columns, 12.; **2.** Students should divide rectangle into 4 rows and 5 columns, 20.; Answers will vary.; Answers will vary but may include trap, pin, car, map, can, and trim.; **3.** gold/fish; **4.** pop/corn; **5.** day/time; **6.** dog/house; **7.** space/ship; **8.** rail/road; **9.** blue/berry; **10.** sail/boat; **11.** grape/fruit; **12.** cup/cake; **13.** news/paper; **14.** some/time

Day 12/Page 83
1. 8; **2.** 1; **3.** 3; **4.** 2; **5.** 4; **6.** 7; **7.** 2; **8.** 4; **9.** 3; **10.** 7; **11.** 8; **12.** 10; **13.** 3; **14.** 4; **15.** 5; **16.** 2:05; **17.** 11:05; **18.** 3:55; **19.** 5:35; **20.** 10:40; **21.** 7:20; 2, 3, 4, 1, Drawings will vary.; **22.** Jonah's; **23.** cat's; **24.** Dante's; **25.** tree's

Day 13/Page 85
1. 23; **2.** 46; **3.** 18; **4.** 54; **5.** 39; **6.** 67; **7.** boy, shoes; **8.** She, letter, aunt; **9.** you, sandwich; **10.** We, movie, butterflies; **11.** sister, ring; January, February, March, April, May, June, July, August, September, October, November, December

Day 14/Page 87
1. 5, 7, 3, 9, 11; **2.** 1, 7, 13, 15, 17; **3.** 5, 11, 9, 13, 17, 19, 3; **4.** 6, 2, 4, 8, 12; **5.** 8, 10, 6, 12, 16; **6.** 14, 16, 12, 18, 4, 8; **7.** sweet; **8.** beach; **9.** boat; **10.** pie; **11.** throw; **12.** play; **13.** coin; **14.** toy; **15.** paw; **16.** daughter; Answers and drawings will vary.

Day 15/Page 89
1. The ferrets lived in the American West.; **2.** The scientists worked to save the ferrets.; **3.** The number of ferrets increased after the scientists started working to save them.; **4.** C; **5.** B; **6.** 1, 0, 1; **7.** 1, 4, 3; **8.** 1, 9, 11; **9.** 9, 3, 2; **10.** you're; **11.** don't; **12.** he's; **13.** I'll; **14.** did not; **15.** is not; **16.** you have; **17.** she is

Day 16/Page 91
1. are; **2.** is; **3.** is; **4.** are; **5.** Is; **6.** Are; **7.** ?; **8.** !; **9.** !; **10.** ?; **11.** .; Answers will vary. **12.** 11; **13.** 12; **14.** 8; **15.** 14; **16.** 9; **17.** 6; **18.** 11; **19.** 7; **20.** 2; **21.** 11; **22.** Students should underline three times the v and d in valentine's day.; **23.** Students should underline three times the t and c in tasty crunch.; **24.** Students should underline three times the l and d in labor day.; **25.** Students should underline three times the c

Answer Key

and n in chicken nibblers.

Day 17/Page 93
1. B; **2.** C; **3.** A; **4.** A; **5.** 18; **6.** 15; **7.** 14; **8.** 14; **9.** 13; **10.** 19; **11.** 15; **12.** 16; **13.** 11; **14.** 11; **15.** ourselves; **16.** themselves; **17.** yourself; **18.** herself; **19.** myself

Day 18/Page 95

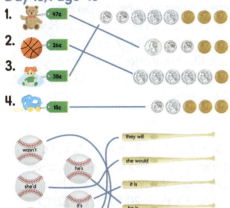

5. B; **6.** A; **7.** C

Day 19/Page 97
1. oak; **2.** six; **3.** funny; **4.** red; **5.** hard; **6.** furry; **7.** A; **8.** A; **9.** Two nickels should be circled.; **10.** A penny, a nickel, and a dime should be circled.; **11.** Two dimes and a nickel should be circled.; **12.** Four dimes and a nickel should be circled.; **13.** not safe; **14.** build again; **15.** not like; **16.** cook before

Day 20/Page 99
1. 6; **2.** 4; **3.** 4; **4.** 12; **5.** 10; **6.** 2; **7.** 5; **8.** 10; **9.** 19; **10.** 2;

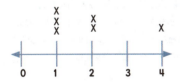

Check students' drawings.; Answers will vary.

Section 3

Day 1/Page 109
1. 15, 18, 17, 19, 13, 14; **2.** 10, 14, 12, 15, 11, 13; **3.** 16, 12, 14, 13, 10, 11; **4.** buy; **5.** light; **6.** once; **7.** carry; **8.** you're; **9.** B; **10.** A; The following words should be written under nose: coat, drove, rope, those.; The following words should be written under pop: rock, fox, job, top.

Day 2/Page 111
1. 4, 0, 2, 5, 6, 3; **2.** 7, 6, 4, 5, 3, 8; **3.** 9, 5, 7, 3, 6, 4; **4.** Roman mowed the yard, but he didn't weed the garden. **5.** Jackson made a fruit salad, and Lena brought dessert.; **6.** The bunny hopped across the yard, but the cat did not see it.; **7.** I could hear the rain on the roof, so I knew the storm had begun.; **8.** Julia walks to school with Chase, or she rides the bus.; **9.** 9 miles; **10.** 9 miles; **11.** no; **12.** yes; **13.** no; **14.** yes; **15.** no; **16.** no;

Day 3/Page 113
1. 41; **2.** 71; **3.** 93; **4.** 81; **5.** 100; **6.** 100; **7.** 90; **8.** 100; **9.** 91; **10.** 62; **11.** 6 cm, 5 cm, 1 cm; **12.** 8 cm, 5 cm, 3 cm; **13.** 0 hundreds, 4 tens, 8 ones, 48; **14.** 1 hundred, 4 tens, 4 ones, 144; **15.** 3 hundreds, 1 ten, 5 ones, 315; **16.** 8 hundreds, 3 tens, 7 ones, 837

Day 4/Page 115
1. 996; **2.** 21; **3.** 82; **4.** 37; **5.** 265; **6.** 661; **7.** 79; **8.** 58; **9.** 22; **10.** 780; **11.** 118; **12.** 100; **13.** 46 inches; **14.** 58 sunflowers; **15.** 92 cans; **16.** $18; **17.** big—little; **18.** slow—fast; **19.** white—black; **20.** This poem is about a missing cat.; **21.** The cat is big, it has white stripes, and it runs fast.

Day 5/Page 117
1. 323; **2.** 517; **3.** 590; **4.** 260; **5.** 393; **6.** 100; The following words should be written under cow: how, brown, clown, tower, crown.; The following words should be written under pillow: blow, elbow, bowl, mow, own.; **7.** A; **8.** E; **9.** F; **10.** C; **11.** B; **12.** D; Answers will vary.

Day 6/Page 119
1. +2; **2.** −2; **3.** +10; **4.** −1; **5.** +5; **6.** −3; **7.** A; **8.** A philatelist is a person who collects stamps.; **9.** There are different ways to get stamps.; **10.** The author wrote it to explain how to collect stamps.

Day 7/Page 121
1. 1; **2.** 2; **3.** 1; **4.** fireworks; **5.** grandfather; **6.** cartwheel; **7.** sunflower; **8.** snowflakes; **9.** waterfall; **10.** 20 (circled), 19, 15, 17; **11.** 16, 19 (circled), 18, 12; **12.** 19 (circled), 10, 13, 16; **13.** 11, 14, 19 (circled), 13; **14.** B, C

Day 8/Page 123
1. about 4 in., about 11 cm; **2.** about 3 in., about 9 cm; **3.** about 2 in., about 5 cm; **4.** about 3 in., about 9 cm; **5.** wash the car; **6.** $7.00; **7.** $0.50; **8.** N; **9.** Y; **10.** Y; **11.** Y;

Answer Key

12. Y; **13.** N; **14.** Y; **15.** N

Day 9/Page 125

1. Three-fourths of the shape should be colored.;
2. One-third of the shape should be colored.; **3.** One-fourth of the shape should be colored.; **4.** Two-thirds of the shape should be colored.; **5.** fruit bowls; **6.** 20 more fruit bowls; **7.** fruit bowls; **8.** 55 students; **9.** 91 shells; **10.** 32 laps; **11.** 84 fish; **12.–14.** Answers will vary.

Day 10/Page 127

1. 6 + 7 = 13, 7 + 6 = 13, 13 – 7 = 6, 13 – 6 = 7; **2.** 7 + 8 = 15, 8 + 7 = 15, 15 – 8 = 7, 15 – 7 = 8; **3.** 10 + 7 = 17, 7 + 10 = 17, 17 – 10 = 7, 17 – 7 = 10; **4.** 6 + 8 = 14, 8 + 6 = 14, 14 – 8 = 6, 14 – 6 = 8; **5.** 7 + 5 = 12, 5 + 7 = 12, 12 – 7 = 5, 12 – 5 = 7; **6.** 5 + 6 = 11, 6 + 5 = 11, 11 – 6 = 5, 11 – 5 = 6; **7.** 21; **8.** 3; **9.** 16; **10.** 6 days

Day 11/Page 129

1. 4 + 4 + 4 + 4 + 4 = 20 or 5 + 5 + 5 + 5 = 20; **2.** 3 + 3 + 3 + 3 = 12 or 4 + 4 + 4 = 12; **3.** 6 + 6 + 6 = 18 or 3 + 3 + 3 + 3 + 3 + 3 = 18; **4.** 4 + 4 + 4 + 4 = 16; **5.** family; **6.** herd; **7.** school; **8.** class; **9.** table; **10.** square; **11.** sky; **12.** light

Day 12/Page 131

1. 12:00; **2.** 9:15; **3.** 2:30; **4.** 4:00; **5.** a/part/ment; **6.** e/nor/mous; **7.** sub/trac/tion; **8.** won/der/ful; **9.** 500; **10.** 900; **11.** 300; **12.** 1,000; **13.** 800; **14.** 700; **15.** 1, 3; **16.** 4, 35; **17.** 6, 57; **18.** 5, 49

Day 13/Page 133

Kate	X	X	X	O
Grace	X	O	X	X
Jade	O	X	X	X
Meghan	X	X	O	X

1. F; **2.** F; **3.** T; **4.** T; **5.** walk; **6.** go; **7.** tired; **8.** full; **9.** B

Day 14/Page 135

1. 600; **2.** 300; **3.** 100; **4.** 200; **5.** 500; **6.** 500; Answers will vary; **7.** 10, 12, 14, 16, 18, 20, +2; **8.** 40, 50, 60, 70, 80, 90, +10; **9.** 20, 25, 30, 35, 40, 45, +5; **10.** 15, 18, 21, 24, 27, 30, +3; Answers will vary.

Day 15/Page 137

1. 9; **2.** 6; **3.** 12; **4.** 15; **5.** 12; **6.** 8; **7.** 20; **8.** 16; **9.** to change

from a liquid into a gas; **10.** camouflage; **11.** dry; **12.** Possible answers: rain and snow; **13.** 2, 5, 1, 200 + 50 + 1; **14.** 3, 4, 1, 300 + 40 + 1; **15.** 5, 6, 3, 500 + 60 + 3; **16.** 7, 5, 2, 700 + 50 + 2; **17.** 65; **18.** 74

Day 16/Page 139

1. B; **2.** After you plant a seed, a tiny seedling pushes its way out.; **3.** Energy comes from food.; **4.** You might need to water your plant if there is little rain where you live.; **5.** The word energy is in bold print because it is important for understanding the text.; **6.** a mayor; **7.** an officer; **8.** a doctor; **9.** a scientist; **10.** an athlete; **11.** an explorer; **12.** an artist; **13.** six; **14.** hairy; **15.** hard; **16.** black; **17.** beautiful; **18.** powerful; **19.** four; **20.** green

Day 17/Page 141

1. <; **2.** >; **3.** >; **4.** <; **5.** <; **6.** >; **7.** <; **8.** <; **9.** <; **10.** >; **11.** >; **12.** <; Answers will vary.; **13.** circle thougt, thought; **14.** circle sents, cents; **15.** circle dragin, dragon; **16.** circle chane, chain; **17.** circle speshal, special; **18.** O; **19.** F; **20.** F; **21.** O; **22.** O **23.** O

Day 18/Page 143

1. C; **2.** The position of the moon as viewed from Earth makes the moon's appearance change.; **3.** A new moon happens when the moon is between the sun and the Earth.; **4.** A; **5.** about 7 cm; **6.** about 9 cm; **7.** about 3 cm; **8.** about 5 cm; **9.** C; **10.** They ran out of flour.

Day 19/Page 145

1. B; **2.** The author says you should take care of your teeth because teeth are important for chewing food.; **3.** Baby teeth fall out and are replaced by adult teeth.; **4.** 32 teeth; **5.** C; **6.** 23; **7.** 20; **8.** 25; **9.** 59; **10.** 28; **11.** 63; **12.** 27; **13.** 63; **14.** 67; **15.** 26; **16.** to take in; **17.** sleepy; **18.** winning; a success; **19.** a rope used for catching livestock; **20.** to knock or push against; **21.** cloudy; **22.** someone who sells things

Day 20/Page 147

1. 3 inches; **2.** 10 inches; **3.** ninth; **4.** 4 inches; **5.** 10 inches; **6.** 11 inches; **7.** proudly, how; **8.** yesterday, when; **9.** outside, where; **10.** safely, how; **11.** ahead, where; **12.** early, when; **13.** 479; **14.** 979; **15.** 376

160

© Carson Dellosa Education

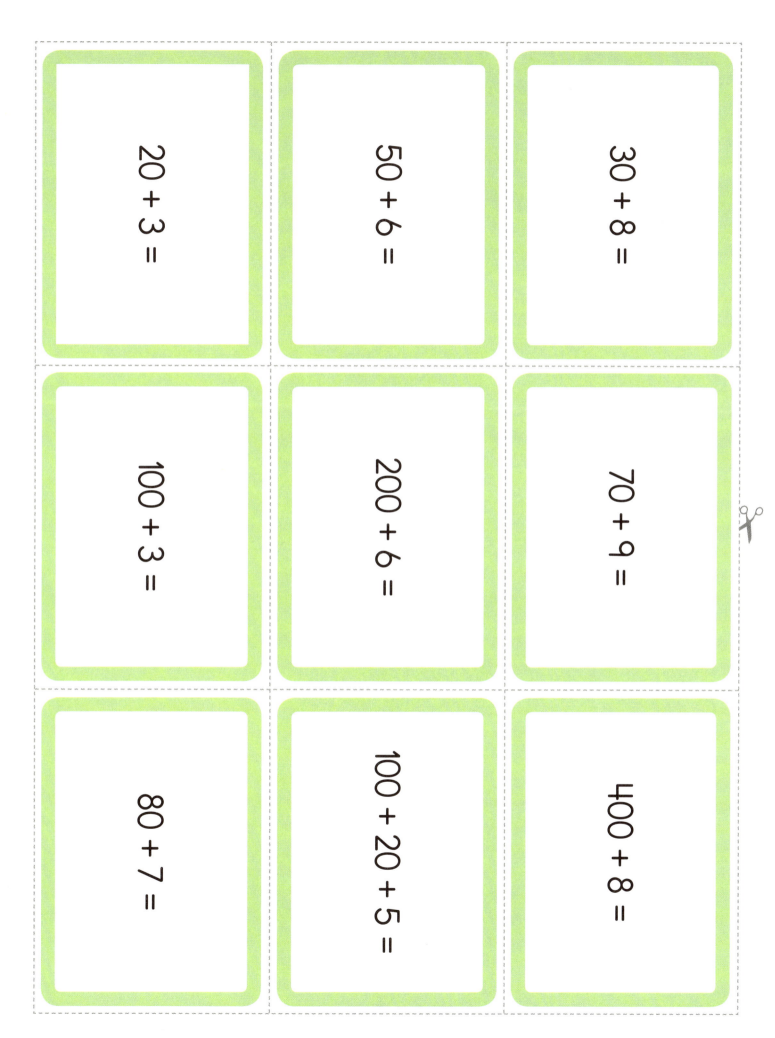

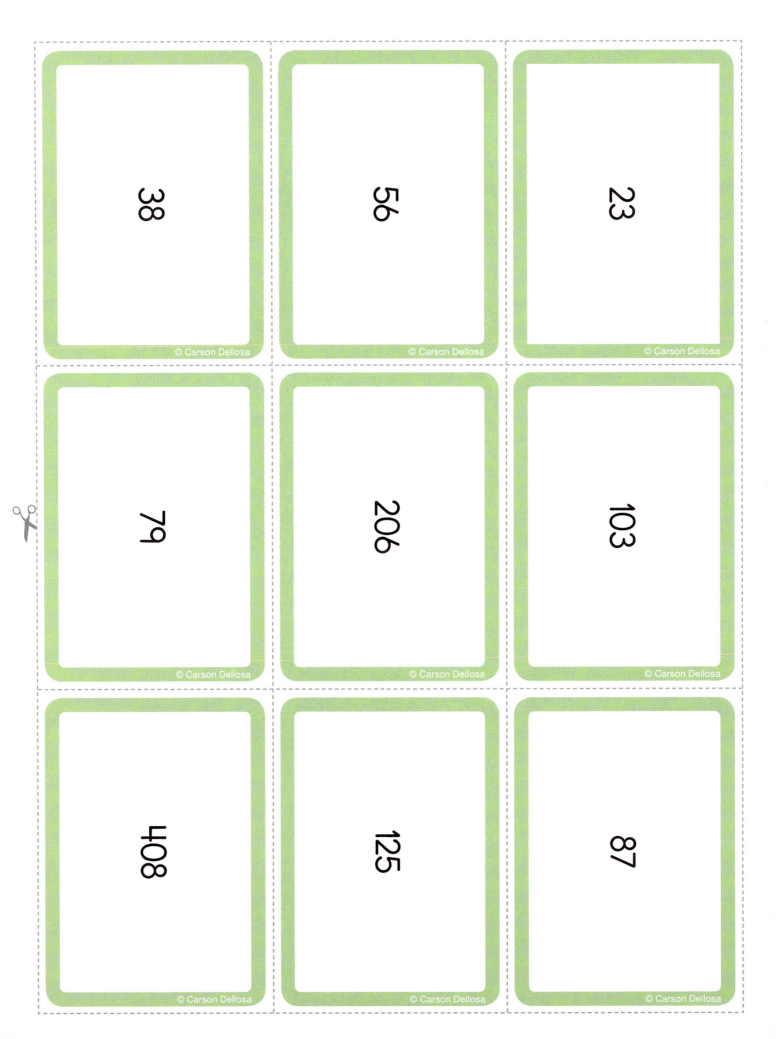

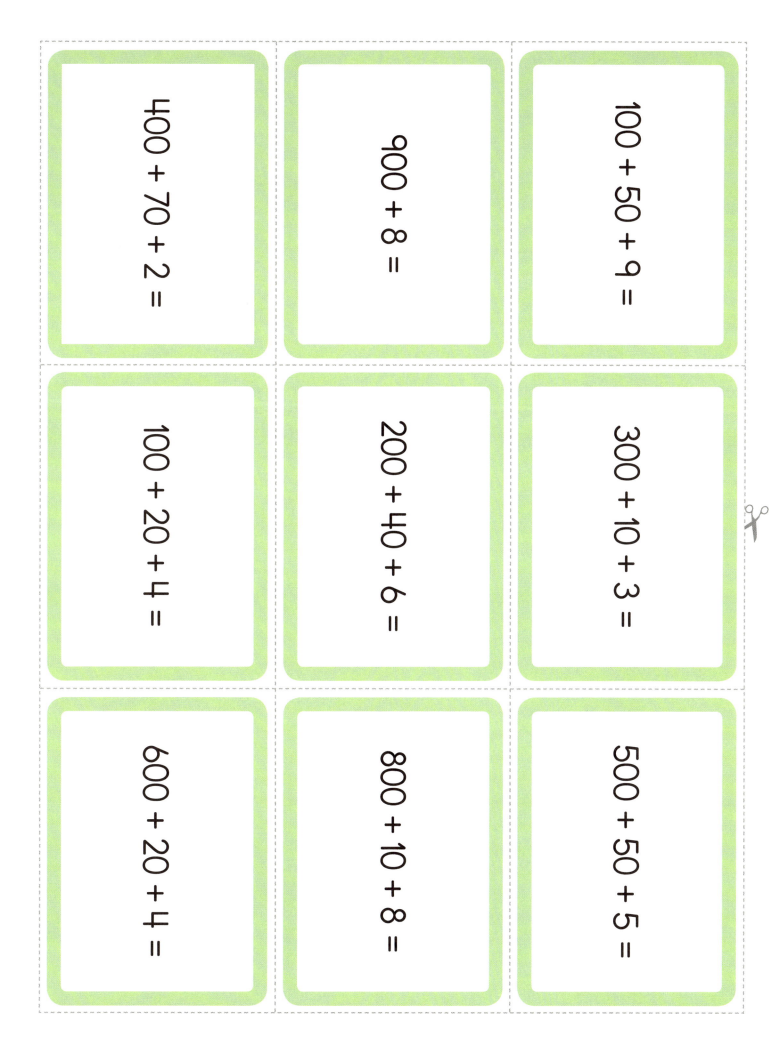

$\begin{array}{r} 11 \\ + 5 \\ \hline \end{array}$	$\begin{array}{r} 9 \\ + 2 \\ \hline \end{array}$	$\begin{array}{r} 10 \\ + 4 \\ \hline \end{array}$
$\begin{array}{r} 12 \\ + 5 \\ \hline \end{array}$	$\begin{array}{r} 10 \\ + 7 \\ \hline \end{array}$	$\begin{array}{r} 8 \\ + 8 \\ \hline \end{array}$
$\begin{array}{r} 10 \\ + 6 \\ \hline \end{array}$	$\begin{array}{r} 13 \\ + 6 \\ \hline \end{array}$	$\begin{array}{r} 10 \\ + 5 \\ \hline \end{array}$

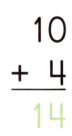

10 + 4 = 14	9 + 2 = 11	11 + 5 = 16
8 + 8 = 16	10 + 7 = 17	12 + 5 = 17
10 + 5 = 15	13 + 6 = 19	10 + 6 = 16

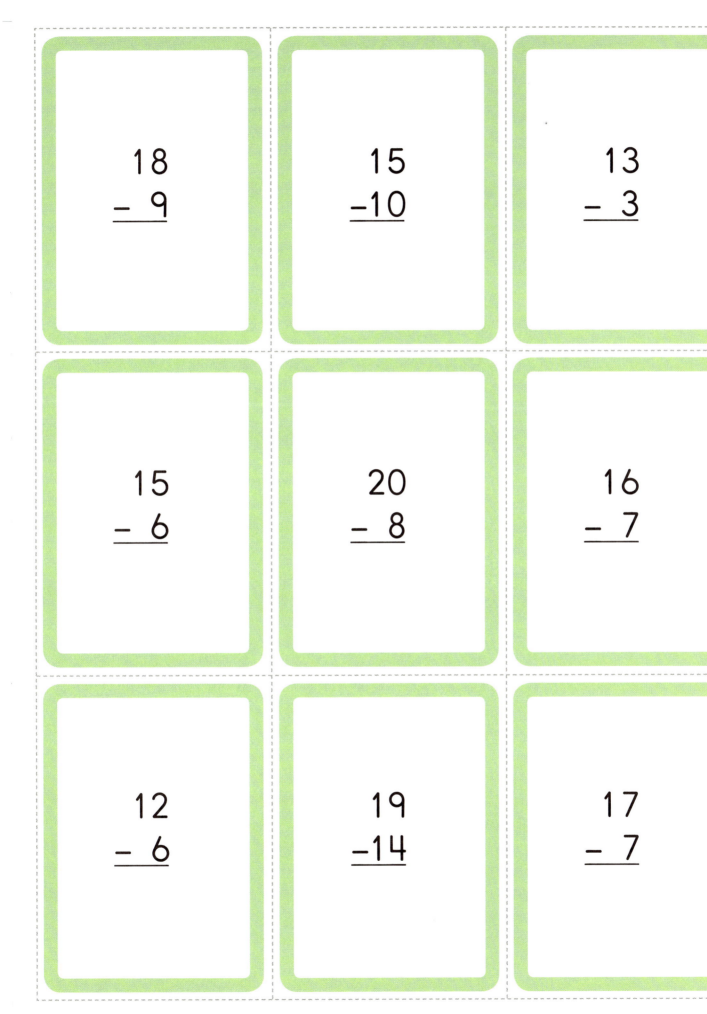

13 − 3 10	15 −10 5	18 − 9 9
16 − 7 9	20 − 8 12	15 − 6 9
17 − 7 10	19 −14 5	12 − 6 6

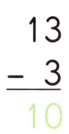

14 − 8	20 −14	16 − 8
13 − 7	20 − 5	11 − 6
14 − 7	18 − 6	19 − 9

16 − 8 **8**	20 −14 **6**	14 − 8 **6**
11 − 6 **5**	20 − 5 **15**	13 − 7 **6**
19 − 9 **10**	18 − 6 **12**	14 − 7 **7**

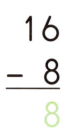

10 + 5 =	13 + 6 =	6 + 10 =
5 + 9 =	11 + 6 =	9 + 9 =
8 + 5 =	7 + 13 =	9 + 7 =

6 + 10 = 16

13 + 6 = 19

10 + 5 = 15

9 + 9 = 18

11 + 6 = 17

5 + 9 = 14

9 + 7 = 16

7 + 13 = 20

8 + 5 = 13

© Carson Dellosa

Cut out the clock pieces and ruler. Use a brass fastener to assemble the clock. Use the clock and ruler to help you solve time and measurement problems in this book.

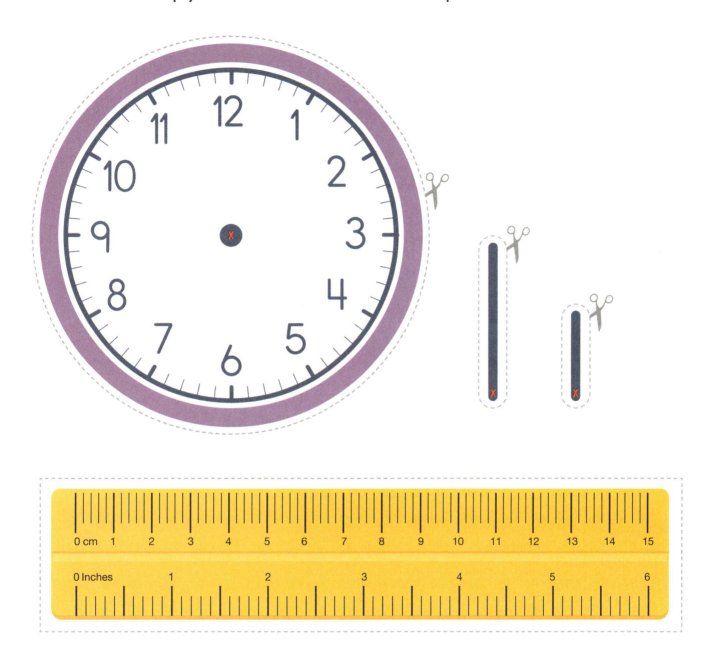

© Carson Dellosa

This page has been intentionally left blank.

Comparing Numbers

Mr. Gator is hungry for lunch.
Find the bigger number and munch, munch, munch!

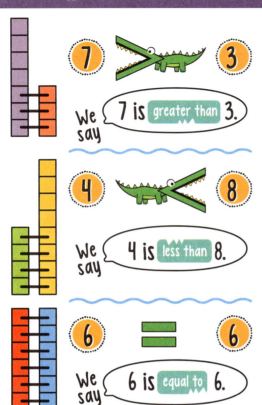

We say 7 is greater than 3.

We say 4 is less than 8.

We say 6 is equal to 6.

Rainbow to 10
HOW MANY WAYS CAN YOU MAKE 10?

0 + 10 = 10   10 + 0 = 10
1 + 9 = 10   9 + 1 = 10
2 + 8 = 10   8 + 2 = 10
3 + 7 = 10   7 + 3 = 10
4 + 6 = 10   6 + 4 = 10
5 + 5 = 10

Units of Time

 60 SECONDS = 1 MINUTE

 60 MINUTES = 1 HOUR

 24 HOURS = 1 DAY

 7 DAYS = 1 WEEK

 52 WEEKS = 1 YEAR
365 DAYS = 1 YEAR
12 MONTHS = 1 YEAR

Identifying Money

Penny 1¢ — one cent $0.01
Nickel 5¢ — five cents $0.05
Dime 10¢ — ten cents $0.10
Quarter 25¢ — twenty-five cents $0.25
Dollar Bill $1.00 — one dollar

SUMMER BUCKET LIST

© Carson Dellosa